ISBN 978-1-331-80914-2
PIBN 10237569

1 MONTH OF
FREE
READING

at

www.ForgottenBooks.com

By purchasing this book you are eligible for one month membership to ForgottenBooks.com, giving you unlimited access to our entire collection of over 700,000 titles via our web site and mobile apps.

To claim your free month visit:

www.forgottenbooks.com/free237569

Similar Books Are Available from
www.forgottenbooks.com

DREAMS

BY

OLIVE SCHREINER

AUTHOR'S EDITION

BOSTON
ROBERTS BROTHERS
1891

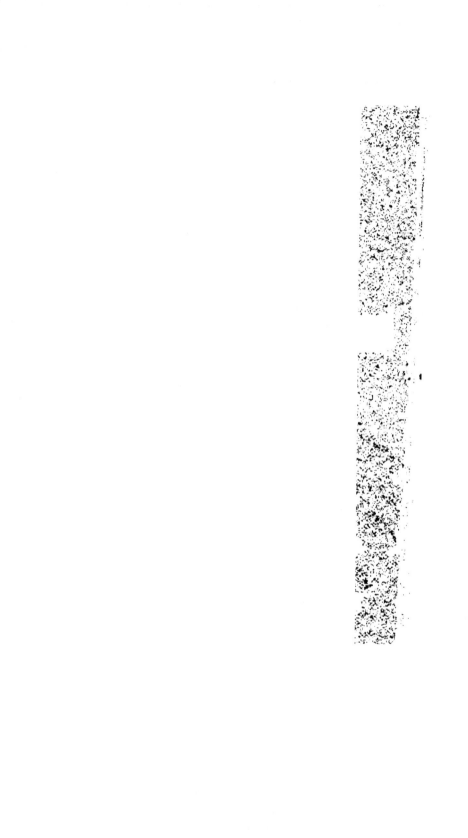

DREAMS

BY

OLIVE SCHREINER

AUTHOR'S EDITION

BOSTON

ROBERTS BROTHERS

1891

Du Maurier's own weakness was Size. Though strong and active, he was but a small man himself, and perhaps on that account his highest admiration, whether for man or beast, was reserved for creatures of colossal proportions. His heroes and heroines must all stand three or four inches over six feet, and their actions must be of the Homeric order. His dog, too, must be of the biggest of his species; and in that matter his desire was gratified by the possession of " Chang," a huge St. Bernard with which all readers of Punch were familiar. When a giant of either sex appeared in London, he would spend all his pocket-money in seeing the monstrosity and treating his friends to a view; and more than once he hinted that if he could have been the real " Gulliver " his happiness would have been complete.

Millais seems to have been a most delightful man in his own family and a most agreeable man in his club. He enjoyed social, but not fashionable, life. His last illness was long and painful. He died, leaving not only a fortune to his family but also a name of which they may well be proud.

The two volumes that go to make up this " Life " would be interesting aside from their 316 illustrations, for they are full of anecdote and reminiscence of the last generation of great writers and painters. Millais knew them all, and what he says about them and what they say of him would make a book that no lover of English letters should leave unread.

Jeannette L. Gilder

To

A SMALL GIRL-CHILD,

WHO MAY LIVE TO GRASP

SOMEWHAT OF THAT WHICH FOR US

IS YET SIGHT, NOT TOUCH.

THE STORY OF AN AFRICAN FARM

FARM

BY RALPH IRON
(*Olive Schreiner*)

Price, 60 cents.

NOTE.

THESE Dreams are printed in the order in which they were written.

In the ease of two there was a lapse of some years between the writing of the first and last parts; these are placed according to the date of the first part.

OLIVE SCHREINER.

MATJESFONTEIN,
CAPE COLONY,
SOUTH AFRICA.
November, 1890.

CONTENTS.

THE LOST JOY.

DREAMS.

THE LOST JOY.

ALL day, where the sunlight played on the sea-shore, Life sat.

All day the soft wind played with her hair, and the young, young face looked out across the water. She was waiting—she was waiting ; but she could not tell for what.

All day the waves ran up and up on the sand, and ran back again, and the pink shells rolled. Life sat waiting ; all day, with the sunlight in her eyes, she sat there, till, grown weary, she laid her head upon her knee and fell asleep, waiting still.

Then a keel grated on the sand, and then a step was on the shore—Life awoke and heard it. A hand was laid upon her, and a great shudder passed through her. She looked up, and saw over her the strange, wide eyes of Love —and Life now knew for whom she had sat there waiting.

And Love drew Life up to him.

And of that meeting was born a thing rare and beautiful—Joy, First-Joy was it called. The sunlight when it shines upon the merry water is not so glad; the rosebuds, when they turn back their lips for the sun's first kiss, are not so ruddy. Its tiny pulses beat quick. It was so warm, so soft! It never spoke, but it laughed and played in the sun- shine : and Love and Life rejoiced exceedingly. Neither whispered it to the other, but deep in its own heart each said, " It shall be ours for ever."

Then there came a time—was it after weeks? was it after months? (Love and Life do not measure time)—when the thing was not as it had been.

Still it played; still it laughed; still it stained its mouth with purple berries; but sometimes the little hands hung weary, and the little eyes looked out heavily across the water.

And Life and Love dared not look into each other's eyes, dared not say, " What ails our darling?" Each heart whispered to itself, " It is nothing, it is nothing, to-morrow it will laugh out clear." But to-morrow and to-morrow came. They journeyed on, and the child played beside them, but heavily, more heavily.

One day Life and Love lay down to

sleep; and when they awoke, it was
gone: only, near them, on the grass,
sat a little stranger, with wide-open
eyes, very soft and sad. Neither
noticed it; but they walked apart,
weeping bitterly, "Oh, our Joy! our
lost Joy! shall we see you no more
for ever?"

The little soft and sad-eyed stranger
slipped a hand into one hand of each,
and drew them closer, and Life and
Love walked on with it between them.
And when Life looked down in anguish,
she saw her tears reflected in its soft
eyes. And when Love, mad with pain,
cried out, "I am weary, I am weary! I
can journey no further. The light is all
behind, the dark is all before," a little
rosy finger pointed where the sunlight
lay upon the hill-sides. Always its large
eyes were sad and thoughtful: always the
little brave mouth was smiling quietly.

When on the sharp stones Life cut her feet, he wiped the blood upon his garments, and kissed the wounded feet with his little lips. When in the desert Love lay down faint (for Love itself grows faint), he ran over the hot sand with his little naked feet, and even there in the desert found water in the holes in the rocks to moisten Love's lips with. He was no burden—he never weighted them; he only helped them forward on their journey.

When they came to the dark ravine where the icicles hang from the rocks— for Love and Life must pass through strange drear places—there, where all is cold, and the snow lies thick, he took their freezing hands and held them against his beating little heart, and warmed them—and softly he drew them on and on.

And when they came beyond, into the

land of sunshine and flowers, strangely
the great eyes lit up, and dimples broke
out upon the face. Brightly laughing,
it ran over the soft grass; gathered
honey from the hollow tree, and brought
it them on the palm of its hand; carried
them water in the leaves of the lily, and
gathered flowers and wreathed them
round their heads, softly laughing all
the while. He touched them as their
Joy had touched them, but his fingers
clung more tenderly.

So they wandered on, through the
dark lands and the light, always with
that little brave smiling one between
them. Sometimes they remembered
that first radiant Joy, and whispered
to themselves, "Oh! could we but
find him also!"

At last they came to where Reflection
sits; that strange old woman who has
always one elbow on her knee, and her

chin in her hand, and who steals light out of the past to shed it on the future.

And Life and Love cried out, "O wise one! tell us : when first we met, a lovely radiant thing belonged to us— gladness without a tear, sunshine without a shade. Oh! how did we sin that we lost it? Where shall we go that we may find it?"

And she, the wise old woman, answered, "To have it back, will you give up that which walks beside you now?"

And in agony Love and Life cried, "No!"

"Give up this!" said Life. "When the thorns have pierced me, who will suck the poison out? When my head throbs, who will lay his tiny hands upon it and still the beating? In the cold and the dark, who will warm my freezing heart?"

And Love cried out, " Better let me die ! Without Joy I can live ; without this I cannot. Let me rather die, not lose it ! "

And the wise old woman answered, "O fools and blind ! What you once had is that which you have now ! When Love and Life first meet, a radiant thing is born, without a shade. When the roads begin to roughen, when the shades begin to darken, when the days are hard, and the nights cold and long— then it begins to change. Love and Life *will* not see it, *will* not know it— till one day they start up suddenly, crying, 'O God ! O God ! we have lost it ! Where is it ?' They do not understand that they could not carry the laughing thing unchanged into the desert, and the frost, and the snow. They do not know that what walks beside them still is the Joy grown older. The grave, sweet, tender thing—warm in the coldest snows, brave in the dreariest deserts—its name is Sympathy; it is the Perfect Love."

South Africa.

THE HUNTER.

THE HUNTER.

N certain valleys there was a hunter. Day by day he went to hunt for wild-fowl in the woods; and it chanced that once he stood on the shores of a large lake. While he stood waiting in the rushes for the coming of the birds, a great shadow fell on him, and in the water he saw a reflection. He looked up to the sky; but the thing was gone. Then a burning desire came over him to see once again that reflection in the water, and all day he watched and waited; but night came, and it had not

returned. Then he went home with his empty bag, moody and silent. His comrades came questioning about him to know the reason, but he answered them nothing; he sat alone and brooded. Then his friend came to him, and to him he spoke.

"I have seen to-day," he said, "that which I never saw before—a vast white bird, with silver wings outstretched, sailing in the everlasting blue. And now it is as though a great fire burnt within my breast. It was but a sheen, a shimmer, a reflection in the water; but now I desire nothing more on earth than to hold her."

His friend laughed.

"It was but a beam playing on the water, or the shadow of your own head. To-morrow you will forget her," he said.

But to-morrow, and to-morrow, and to-morrow the hunter walked alone. He sought in the forest and in the woods, by the lakes and among the rushes, but he could not find her. He shot no more wild-fowl; what were they to him?

"What ails him?" said his comrades.

"He is mad," said one.

"No, but he is worse," said another; "he would see that which none of us have seen, and make himself a wonder."

"Come, let us forswear his company," said all.

So the hunter walked alone.

One night, as he wandered in the shade, very heart-sore and weeping, an old man stood before him, grander and taller than the sons of men.

"Who are you?" asked the hunter.

"I am Wisdom," answered the old man; "but some men called me Knowledge. All my life I have grown in these valleys; but no·man sees me till he has sorrowed much. The eyes must be washed with tears that are to behold me ; and, according as a man has suffered, I speak."

And the hunter cried—

" Oh, you who have lived here so long, tell me, what is that great wild bird I have seen sailing in the blue ? They would have me believe she is a dream ; the shadow of my own head."

The old man smiled.

" Her name is Truth. He who has once seen her never rests again. Till death he desires her."

And the hunter cried—

" Oh, tell me where I may find her."

But the man said,

" You have not suffered enough," and went.

Then the hunter took from his breast the shuttle of Imagination, and wound on it the thread of his Wishes; and all night he sat and wove a net.

In the morning he spread the golden net open on the ground, and into it he threw a few grains of credulity, which his father had left him, and which he kept in his breast-pocket. They were like white puff-balls, and when you trod on them a brown dust flew out. Then he sat by to see what would happen. The first that came into the net was a snow-white bird, with dove's eyes, and he sang a beautiful song—"A human-God! a human-God! a human-God!" it sang. The second that came was black and mystical, with dark, lovely eyes, that looked into the depths of your soul, and he sang only this—"Immortality!"

And the hunter took them both in his arms, for he said—

"They are surely of the beautiful family of Truth."

Then came another, green and gold, who sang in a shrill voice, like one crying in the market-place,—" Reward after Death! Reward after Death!"

And he said—

" You are not so fair; but you are fair too," and he took it.

And others came, brightly coloured, singing pleasant songs, till all the grains were finished. And the hunter gathered all his birds together, and built a strong iron cage called a new creed, and put all his birds in it.

Then the people came about dancing and singing.

" Oh, happy hunter!" they cried. " Oh, wonderful man! Oh, delightful birds! Oh, lovely songs!"

No one asked where the birds had come from, nor how they had been caught; but they danced and sang before them And the hunter too was glad, for he said—

"Surely Truth is among them. In time she will moult her feathers, and I shall see her snow-white form."

But the time passed, and the people sang and danced ; but the hunter's heart grew heavy. He crept alone, as of old, to weep ; the terrible desire had awakened again in his breast. One day, as he sat alone weeping, it chanced that Wisdom met him. He told the old man what he had done.

And Wisdom smiled sadly.

" Many men," he said, " have spread that net for Truth ; but they have never found her. On the grains of credulity she will not feed ; in the net of wishes her feet cannot be held ; in the air of these valleys she will not breathe. The birds you have caught are of the brood of Lies. Lovely and beautiful, but still lies ; Truth knows them not."

And the hunter cried out in bitterness—·

"And must I then sit still to be devoured of this great burning ?"

And the old man said—

"Listen, and in that you have suffered much and wept much, I will tell you what I know. He who sets out to search for Truth must leave these valleys of superstition for ever, taking with him not one shred that has belonged to them. Alone he must wander down into the Land of Absolute Negation and Denial; he must abide there; he must resist temptation; when the light breaks he must arise and follow it into the country of dry sunshine. The mountains of stern reality will rise before him; he must climb them; *beyond* them lies Truth."

"And he will hold her fast! he will hold her in his hands!" the hunter cried.

Wisdom shook his head.

"He will never see her, never hold her. The time is not yet."

"Then there is no hope?" cried the hunter.

"There is this," said Wisdom. "Some men have climbed on those mountains; circle above circle of bare rock they have scaled; and, wandering there, in those high regions, some have chanced to pick up on the ground, one white, silver feather dropped from the wing of Truth. And it shall come to pass," said the old man, raising himself prophetically and pointing with his finger to the sky, "it shall come to pass, that, when enough of those silver feathers shall have been gathered by the hands of men, and shall have been woven into a cord, and the cord into a net, that in *that* net Truth may be captured. *Nothing but Truth can hold Truth.*"

The hunter arose. "I will go," he said.

But Wisdom detained him.

" Mark you well—who leaves these valleys *never* returns to them. Though he should weep tears of blood seven days and nights upon the confines, he can never put his foot across them. Left — they are left for ever. Upon the road which you would travel there is no reward offered. Who goes, goes freely—for the great love that is in him. The work is his reward."

" I go," said the hunter ; "but upon the mountains, tell me, which path shall I take ? "

" I am the child of The-Accumulated-Knowledge-of-Ages," said the man; " I can walk only where many men have trodden. On these mountains few feet have passed ; each man strikes out a path for himself. He goes at his own peril : my voice he hears no more I may follow after him, but I cannot go before him."

Then Knowledge vanished.

And the hunter turned. He went to his cage, and with his hands broke down the bars, and the jagged iron tore his flesh. It is sometimes easier to build than to break.

One by one he took his plumed birds and let them fly. But, when he came to his dark-plumed bird, he held it, and looked into its beautiful eyes, and the bird uttered its low deep cry—" Immortality!"

And he said quickly, " I cannot part with it. It is not heavy; it eats no food. I will hide it in my breast: I will take it with me." And he buried it there, and covered it over with his cloak.

But the thing he had hidden grew heavier, heavier, heavier—till it lay on his breast like lead. He could not move with it. He could not leave those valleys with it   Then again he took it out and looked at it.

"Oh, my beautiful, my heart's own !" he cried, "may I not keep you ?"

He opened his hands sadly.

"Go," he said.   "It may happen that in Truth's song one note is like to yours ; but *I* shall never hear it."

Sadly he opened his hand, and the bird flew from him for ever.

Then from the shuttle of Imagination he took the thread of his wishes, and threw it on the ground ; and the empty shuttle he put into his breast, for the thread was made in those valleys, but the shuttle came from an unknown country.   He turned to go, but now the people came about him, howling.

"Fool, hound, demented lunatic!" they cried. "How dared you break your cage and let the birds fly ?"

The hunter spoke ; but they would not hear him.

" Truth! who is she? Can you eat her? can you drink her? Who has ever seen her? Your birds were real · all could hear them sing! Oh, fool! vile reptile! atheist!" they cried, "you pollute the air."

" Come, let us take up stones and stone him," cried some.

" What affair is it of ours?" said others. " Let the idiot go;" and went away. But the rest gathered up stones and mud and threw at him. At last, when he was bruised and cut, the hunter crept away into the woods. And it was evening about him.

He wandered on and on, and the shade grew deeper. He was on the borders now of the land where it is always night. Then he stepped into it, and there was no light there. With his hands he groped; but each branch as he touched it broke

off, and the earth was covered with
cinders. At every step his foot sank
in, and a fine cloud of impalpable ashes
flew up into his face ; and it was dark.
So he sat down upon a stone and
buried his face in his hands, to wait
in that Land of Negation and Denial
till the light came.

And it was night in his heart also.

Then from the marshes to his right
and left cold mists arose and closed
about him. A fine, imperceptible rain
fell in the dark, and great drops gathered
on his hair and clothes. His heart beat
slowly, and a numbness crept through
all his limbs. Then, looking up, two
merry wisp lights came dancing. He
lifted his head to look at them. Nearer,
nearer they came. So warm, so bright,
they danced like stars of fire. They
stood before him at last. From the
centre of the radiating flame in one

looked out a woman's face, laughing, dimpled, with streaming yellow hair. In the centre of the other were merry laughing ripples, like the bubbles on a glass of wine. They danced before him.

"Who are you," asked the hunter, "who alone come to me in my solitude and darkness?"

"We are the twins Sensuality," they cried. "Our father's name is Human-Nature, and our mother's name is Excess. We are as old as the hills and rivers, as old as the first man; but we never die," they laughed.

"Oh, let me wrap my arms about you!" cried the first; "they are soft and warm. Your heart is frozen now, but I will make it beat. Oh, come to me!"

"I will pour my hot life into you," said the second; "your brain is numb, and your limbs are dead now; but they shall live with a fierce free life. Oh, let me pour it in!"

"Oh, follow us," they cried, "and live with us. Nobler hearts than yours have sat here in this darkness to wait, and they have come to us and we to them; and they have never left us, never. All else is a delusion, but *we* are real, we are real. Truth is a shadow; the valleys of superstition are a farce; the earth is of ashes, the trees all rotten; but we—feel us—we live! You cannot doubt us. Feel us, how warm we are! Oh, come to us! Come with us!"

Nearer and nearer round his head they hovered, and the cold drops melted on his forehead. The bright light shot into his eyes, dazzling him, and the frozen blood began to run. And he said—

"Yes; why should I die here in this

awful darkness? They are warm, they melt my frozen blood!" and he stretched out his hands to take them.

Then in a moment there arose before him the image of the thing he had loved, and his hand dropped to his side.

"Oh, come to us!" they cried.

But he buried his face.

"You dazzle my eyes," he cried, "you make my heart warm; but you cannot give me what I desire. I will wait here—wait till I die. Go!"

He covered his face with his hands and would not listen; and when he looked up again they were two twinkling stars, that vanished in the distance.

And the long, long night rolled on.

All who leave the valley of superstition pass through that dark land; but some go through it in a few days, some linger there for months, some for years, and some die there.

At last for the hunter a faint light played along the horizon, and he rose to follow it ; and he reached that light at last, and stepped into the broad sunshine. Then before him rose the almighty mountains of Dry-facts and Realities. The clear sunshine played on them, and the tops were lost in the clouds At the foot many paths ran up. An exultant cry burst from the hunter. He chose the straightest and began to climb ; and the rocks and ridges resounded with his song. They had exaggerated ; after all, it was not so high, nor was the road so steep! A few days, a few weeks, a few months at most, and then the top! Not one feather only would he pick up; he would gather all that other men had found—weave the net—capture Truth

—hold her fast—touch her with his hands—clasp her!

He laughed in the merry sunshine, and sang loud. Victory was very near. Nevertheless, after a while the path grew steeper. He needed all his breath for climbing, and the singing died away. On the right and left rose huge rocks, devoid of lichen or moss, and in the lava-like earth chasms yawned. Here and there he saw a sheen of white bones. Now too the path began to grow less and less marked; then it became a mere trace, with a foot-mark here and there; then it ceased altogether. He sang no more, but struck forth a path for himself, until he reached a mighty wall of rock, smooth and without break, stretching as far as the eye could see. " I will rear a stair against it; and, once this wall climbed, I shall be almost there," he said bravely; and worked. With his shuttle of imagination he dug out stones; but half of them would not fit, and half a month's work would roll down because those below were ill chosen. But the hunter worked on, saying always to to himself, "Once this wall climbed, I shall be almost there. This great work ended!"

At last he came out upon the top, and he looked about him. Far below rolled the white mist over the valleys of superstition, and above him towered the mountains. They had seemed low before; they were of an immeasurable height now, from crown to foundation surrounded by walls of rock, that rose tier above tier in mighty circles. Upon them played the eternal sunshine. He uttered a wild cry. He bowed himself on to the earth, and when he rose his face was white. In absolute silence he walked on. He was very silent now. In those high regions the rarefied air is hard to breathe by those born in the valleys; every breath he drew hurt him, and the blood oozed out from the tips of his fingers. Before the next wall of rock he began to work. The height of this seemed infinite, and he said nothing. The sound of his tool rang night and day upon the iron rocks into which he cut steps. Years passed over him, yet he worked on; but the wall towered up always above him to heaven. Sometimes he prayed that a little moss or lichen might spring up on those bare walls to be a companion to him; but it never came.

And the years rolled on: he counted them by the steps he had cut—a few for a year—only a few. He sang no more; he said no more, " I will do this or that "—he only worked. And at night, when the twilight settled down, there looked out at him from the holes and crevices in the rocks strange wild faces.

"Stop your work, you lonely man, and speak to us," they cried.

"My salvation is in work. If I should stop but for one moment you would creep down upon me," he replied. And they put out their long necks further.

"Look down into the crevice at your feet," they said. "See what lie there— white bones! As brave and strong a man as you climbed to these rocks. And he looked up. He saw there was no use in striving; he would never hold Truth, never see her, never find her. So he lay down here, for he was very tired. He went to sleep for ever. He put himself to sleep. Sleep is very tranquil. You are not lonely when you are asleep, neither do your hands ache, nor your heart." And ·the hunter laughed between his teeth.

" Have I torn from my heart all that was dearest; have I wandered alone in the land of night; have I resisted temptation; have I dwelt where the voice of my kind is never heard, and laboured alone, to lie down and be food for you, ye harpies?"

He laughed fiercely; and the Echoes of Despair slunk away, for the laugh of a brave, strong heart is as a death-blow to them.

Nevertheless they crept out again and looked at him.

" Do you know that your hair is white?" they said, "that your hands begin to tremble like a child's? Do you see that the point of your shuttle is gone?—it is cracked already. If you should ever climb this stair," they said, "it will be your last. You will never climb another."

And he answered, "*I know it!*" and worked on.

The old, thin hands cut the stones ill and jaggedly, for the fingers were stiff and bent. The beauty and the strength of the man was gone.

At last, an old, wizened, shrunken face looked out above the rocks. It saw the eternal mountains rise with walls to the white clouds; but its work was done.

The old hunter folded his tired hands and lay down by the precipice where he had worked away his life. It was the sleeping time at last. Below him over the valleys rolled the thick white mist. Once it broke; and through the gap the dying eyes looked down on the trees and fields of their childhood. From afar seemed borne to him the cry of his own wild birds, and he heard the noise of people singing as they danced. And he thought he heard among them the voices of his old com rades; and he saw far off the sunlight shine on his early home. And great tears gathered in the hunter's eyes.

"Ah! they who die there do not die alone," he cried.

Then the mists rolled together again; and he turned his eyes away.

"I have sought," he said, "for long years I have laboured; but I have not found her. I have not rested, I have not repined, and I have not seen her; now my strength is gone. Where I lie down worn out, other men will stand, young and fresh. By the steps that I have cut they will climb; by the stairs that I have built, they will mount. They will never know the name of the man who made them. At the clumsy work they will laugh; when the stones roll they will curse me.   But they will mount, and on *my* work ; they will climb, and by *my* stair ! They will find her, and ·through me ! And no man liveth to himself, and no man dieth to himself."

The tears rolled from beneath the shrivelled eyelids.   If Truth had appeared above him in the clouds now he could not have seen her, the mist of death was in his eyes.

"My soul hears their glad step coming," he said ; "and they shall mount! they shall mount!"   He raised his shrivelled hand to his eyes.

Then slowly from the white sky above, through the still air, came something falling, falling, falling.   Softly it fluttered down, and dropped on to the breast of the dying man.   He felt it with his hands.   It was a feather.   He died holding it.

THE GARDENS OF PLEASURE.

THE GARDENS OF PLEASURE.

SHE walked upon the beds, and the sweet rich scent arose; and she gathered her hands full of flowers. Then Duty, with his white clear features, came and looked at her. Then she ceased from gathering, but she walked away among the flowers, smiling, and with her hands full.

Then Duty, with his still white face, came again, and looked at her; but she, she turned her head away from him. At last she saw his face, and she dropped the fairest of the flowers she had held, and walked silently away.

Then again he came to her. And she moaned, and bent her head low, and turned to the gate. But as she went out she looked back at the sunlight on the faces of the flowers, and wept in anguish. Then she went out, and it shut behind her for ever; but still in her hand she held of the buds she had gathered, and the scent was very sweet in the lonely desert.

But he followed her. Once more he stood before her with his still, white, death-like face. And she knew what he had come for: she unbent the fingers, and let the flowers drop out, the flowers she had loved so, and walked on without them, with dry, aching eyes. Then for the last time he came. And she showed him her empty hands, the hands that held nothing now. But still he looked.

Then at length she opened her bosom and took out of it one small flower she had hidden there, and laid it on the sand. She had nothing more to give now, and she wandered away, and the grey sand whirled about her.

IN A FAR-OFF WORLD.

IN A FAR-OFF WORLD.

HERE is a world in one of the far-off stars, and things do not happen here as they happen there.

In that world were a man and woman; they had one work, and they walked together side by side on many days, and were friends—and that is a thing that happens now and then in this world also.

But there was something in that star-world that there is not here. There was a thick wood : where the trees grew closest, and the stems were interlocked, and the summer sun never shone, there stood a shrine. In the day all was quiet, but at night, when the stars shone or the moon glinted on the tree-tops, and all was quiet below, if one crept here quite alone and knelt on the steps of the stone altar, and uncovering one's breast, so wounded it that the blood fell down on the altar steps, then whatever he who knelt there wished for was granted him   And all this happens, as I said, because it is a far-off world, and things often happen there as they do not happen here.

Now, the man and woman walked together; and the woman wished well to the man.   One night when the moon was shining so that the leaves of all the trees glinted, and the waves of the sea were silvery, the woman walked alone to the forest.   It was dark there; the moonlight fell only in little flecks on the dead leaves under her feet, and the branches were knotted tight overhead. Farther in it got darker, not even a fleck of moonlight shone. Then she came to the shrine; she knelt down before it and prayed; there came no answer. Then she uncovered her breast; with a sharp two-edged stone that lay there she wounded it. The drops dripped slowly down on to the stone, and a voice cried, " What do you seek ? "

She answered, " There is a man; I hold him nearer than anything. I would give him the best of all blessings."

The voice said, " What is it ? "

The girl said, " I know not, but that which is most good for him I wish him to have."

The voice said, " Your prayer is answered; he shall have it."

Then she stood up. She covered her
breast and held the garment tight upon
it with her hand, and ran out of the
forest, and the dead leaves fluttered
under her feet. Out in the moonlight
the soft air was blowing, and the sand
glittered on the beach. She ran along
the smooth shore, then suddenly she
stood still. Out across the water there
was something moving. She shaded
her eyes and looked. It was a boat;
it was sliding swiftly over the moonlit
water out to sea. One stood upright in
it; the face the moonlight did not show,
but the figure she knew. It was pass-
ing swiftly; it seemed as if no one
propelled it; the moonlight's shimmer
did not let her see clearly, and the boat
was far from shore, but it seemed almost
as if there was another figure sitting in
the stern. Faster and faster it glided
over the water away, away. She ran

along the shore ; she came no nearer it. The garment she had held closed fluttered open ; she stretched out her arms, and the moonlight shone on her long loose hair.

Then a voice beside her whispered, "What is it ? "

She cried, "With my blood I bought the best of all gifts for him. I have come to bring it him ! He is going from me ! "

The voice whispered softly, " Your prayer was answered. It has been given him."

She cried, "What is it ? "

The voice answered, " It is that he might leave you."

The girl stood still.

Far out at sea the boat was lost to sight beyond the moonlight sheen.

The voice spoke softly, " Art thou contented ? "

She said, " I am contented."

At her feet the waves broke in long ripples softly on the shore.

THREE DREAMS IN A DESERT.

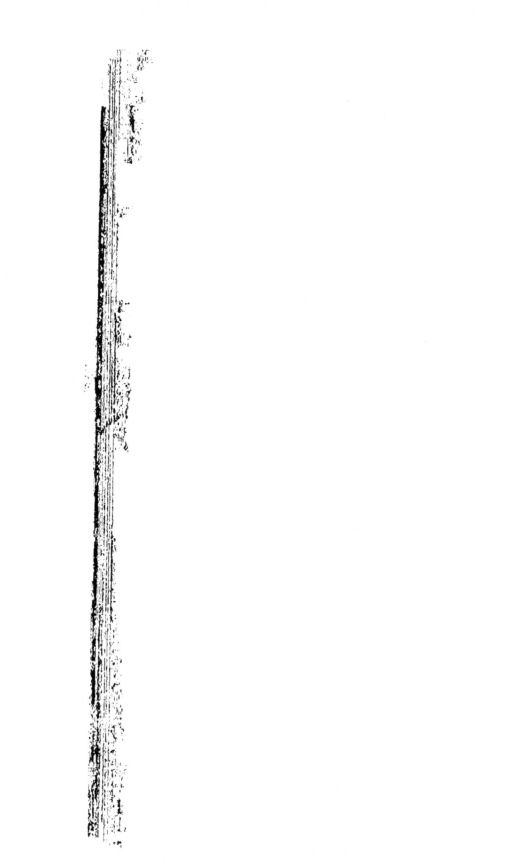

THREE DREAMS IN A DESERT.

UNDER A MIMOSA-TREE.

AS I travelled across an African plain the sun shone down hotly. Then I drew my horse up under a mimosa-tree, and I took the saddle from him and left him to feed among the parched bushes And all to right and to left stretched the brown earth. And I sat down under the tree, because the heat beat fiercely, and all along the horizon the air throbbed. And after a while a heavy drowsiness came over me, and I laid my head down against my saddle, and I fell asleep there   And, in my sleep, I had a curious dream.

I thought I stood on the border of a great desert, and the sand blew about everywhere.   And I thought I saw two great figures like beasts of burden of the desert, and one lay upon the sand with its neck stretched out, and one stood by it.   And I looked curiously at the one that lay upon the ground, for it had a great burden on its back, and the sand was thick about it, so that it seemed to have piled over it for centuries.

And I looked very curiously at it. And there stood one beside me watching.   And I said to him, " What is this huge creature who lies here on the sand ? "

And he said, " This is woman ; she that bears men in her body."

And I said, " Why does she lie here

motionless with the sand piled round her?"

And he answered, " Listen, I will tell you! Ages and ages long she has lain here, and the wind has blown over her. The oldest, oldest, oldest man living has never seen her move: the oldest, oldest book records that she lay here then, as she lies here now, with the sand about her. But listen! Older than the oldest book, older than the oldest recorded memory of man, on the Rocks of Language, on the hard-baked clay of Ancient Customs, now crumbling to decay, are found the marks of her footsteps! Side by side with his who stands beside her you may trace them; and you know that she who now lies there once wandered free over the rocks with him."

And I said, "Why does she lie there now?"

And he said, " I take it, ages ago the Age-of-dominion-of-muscular-force found her, and when she stooped low to give suck to her young, and her back was broad, he put his burden of subjection on to it, and tied it on with the broad band of Inevitable Necessity. Then she looked at the earth and the sky, and knew there was no hope for her; and she lay down on the sand with the burden she could not loosen. Ever since she has lain here. And the ages have come, and the ages have gone, but the band of Inevitable Necessity has not been cut."

And I looked and saw in her eyes the terrible patience of the centuries; the ground was wet with her tears, and her nostrils blew up the sand.

And I said, " Has she ever tried to move ? "

And he said, " Sometimes a limb has

quivered. But she is wise ; she knows she cannot rise with the burden on her."

And I said, "Why does not he who stands by her leave her and go on ?"

And he said, "He cannot. Look——"

And I saw a broad band passing along the ground from one to the other, and it bound them together.

He said, "While she lies there he must stand and look across the desert."

And I said, " Does he know why he cannot move ? "

And he said, " No."

And I heard a sound of something cracking, and I looked, and I saw the band that bound the burden on to her back broken asunder ; and the burden rolled on to the ground.

And I said, "What is this ? "

And he said, " The Age-of-muscular-force is dead. The Age-of-nervous-force has killed him with the knife he holds in his hand; and silently and invisibly he has crept up to the woman, and with that knife of Mechanical Invention he has cut the band that bound the burden to her back. The Inevitable Necessity is broken. She might rise now."

And I saw that she still lay motionless on the sand, with her eyes open and her neck stretched out. And she seemed to look for something on the far-off border of the desert that never came And I wondered if she were awake or asleep, And as I looked her body quivered, and a light came into her eyes, like when a sunbeam breaks into a dark room.

I said, "What is it?"

He whispered "Hush! the thought has come to her, ' Might I not rise?'"

And I looked. And she raised her head from the sand, and I saw the dent where her neck had lain so long. And she looked at the earth, and she looked at the sky, and she looked at him who stood by her : but he looked out across the desert.

And I saw her body quiver ; and she pressed her front knees to the earth, and veins stood out ; and I cried, " She is going to rise ! "

But only her sides heaved, and she lay still where she was.

But her head she held up ; she did not lay it down again. And he beside me said, " She is very weak. See, her legs have been crushed under her so long."

And I saw the creature struggle : and the drops stood out on her.

And I said, " Surely he who stands beside her will help her ? "

And he beside me answered, " He cannot help her : *she must help herself.* Let her struggle till she is strong."

And I cried, "At least he will not hinder her! See, he moves farther from her, and tightens the cord between them, and he drags her down."

And he answered, "He does not understand. When she moves she draws the band that binds them, and hurts him, and he moves farther from her. The day will come when he will understand, and will know what she is doing. Let her once stagger on to her knees. In that day he will stand close to her, and look into her eyes with sympathy."

And she stretched her neck, and the drops fell from her. And the creature rose an inch from the earth and sank back.

And I cried, "Oh, she is too weak! she cannot walk! The long years have taken all her strength from her. Can she never move?"

And he answered me, "See the light in her eyes!"

And slowly the creature staggered on to its knees.

And I awoke : and all to the east and to the west stretched the barren earth, with the dry bushes on it. The ants ran up and down in the red sand, and the heat beat fiercely. I looked up through the thin branches of the tree at the blue sky overhead. I stretched myself, and I mused over the dream I had had. And I fell asleep again, with my head on my saddle. And in the fierce heat I had another dream.

I saw a desert and I saw a woman coming out of it. And she came to the bank of a dark river ; and the bank was steep and high.[1] And on it an old

---

[1] The banks of an African river are sometimes a hundred feet high, and consist of deep shifting sands, through which in the course of ages the river has worn its gigantic bed.

man met her, who had a long white
beard; and a stick that curled was in
his hand, and on it was written Reason.
And he asked her what she wanted;
and she said "I am woman; and I am
seeking for the land of Freedom."

And he said, "It is before you."

And she said, "I see nothing before
me but a dark flowing river, and a bank
steep and high, and cuttings here and
there with heavy sand in them."

And he said, "And beyond that?"

She said, "I see nothing, but some-
times, when I shade my eyes with my
hand, I think I see on the further bank
trees and hills, and the sun shining on
them!"

He said, "That is the Land of
Freedom."

She said, "How am I to get there?"

He said, "There is one way, and one
only   Down the banks of Labour,

through the water of Suffering. There is no other."

She said, " Is there no bridge ? "

He answered. " None."

She said, " Is the water deep ? "

He said, " Deep."

She said, " Is the floor worn ? "

He said, " It is. Your foot may slip at any time, and you may be lost."

She said, "Have any crossed already?"

He said, " Some have *tried* ! "

She said, " Is there a track to show where the best fording is ? "

He said, " It has to be made."

She shaded her eyes with her hand; and she said, " I will go."

And he said, " You must take off the clothes you wore in the desert: they are dragged down by them who go into the water so clothed."

And she threw from her gladly the mantle of Ancient-received-opinions she wore, for it was worn full of holes. And she took the girdle from her waist that she had treasured so long, and the moths flew out of it in a cloud. And he said, " Take the shoes of dependence off your feet."

And she stood there naked, but for one white garment that clung close to her.

And he said, " That you may keep. So they wear clothes in the Land of Freedom. In the water it buoys; it always swims."

And I saw on its breast was written Truth ; and it was white ; the sun had not often shone on it ; the other clothes had covered it up. And he said, " Take this stick; hold it fast. In that day when it slips from your hand you are lost. Put it down before you; feel your way : where it cannot find a bottom do not set your foot."

And she said, " I am ready ; let me go."

And he said, " No—but stay ; what is that—in your breast ? "

She was silent.

He said, " Open it, and let me see."

And she opened it. And against her breast was a tiny thing, who drank from it, and the yellow curls above his forehead pressed against it ; and his knees were drawn up to her, and he held her breast fast with his hands.

And Reason said, " Who is he, and what is he doing here ? "

And she said, "See his little wings——

And Reason said, " Put him down."

And she said, " He is asleep, and he is drinking! I will carry him to the Land of Freedom. He has been a child so long, so long, I have carried him. In the Land of Freedom he will be a man. We will walk together there, and his great white wings will overshadow me. He has lisped one word only to me in the desert— ' Passion!' I have dreamed he might learn to say ' Friendship ' in that land."

And Reason said, " Put him down!"

And she said, " I will carry him so— with one arm, and with the other I will fight the water."

He said, " Lay him down on the ground. When you are in the water you will forget to fight, you will think only of him. Lay him down." He said, " He will not die. When he finds you have left him alone he will open his wings and fly. He will be in the Land of Freedom before you. Those who reach the Land of Freedom, the first hand they see stretching down the bank to help them shall be Love's. He will be a man then, not a child. In your breast he cannot thrive ; pu down that he may grow."

And she took her bosom from his mouth, and he bit her, so that the blood ran down on to the ground. And she laid him down on the earth ; and she covered her wound. And she bent and stroked his wings. And I saw the hair on her forehead turned white as snow, and she had changed from youth to age.

And she stood far off on the bank of the river. And she said, " For what do I go to this far land which no one has ever reached? *Oh, I am alone! I am utterly alone !* "

And Reason, that old man, said to her, " Silence ! what do you hear ? "

And she listened intently, and she said, " I hear a sound of feet, a thousand times ten thousand and thousands of thousands, and they beat this way!"

He said, "They are the feet of those that shall follow you. Lead on! make a track to the water's edge! Where you stand now, the ground will be beaten flat by ten thousand times ten thousand feet." And he said, "Have you seen the locusts how they cross a stream? First one comes down to the water-edge, and it is swept away, and then another comes and then another, and then another, and at last with their bodies piled up a bridge is built and the rest pass over."

She said, "And, of those that come first, some are swept away, and are heard of no more; their bodies do not even build the bridge?"

"And are swept away, and are heard of no more—and what of that?" he said.

" And what of that——" she said.

" They make a track to the water's edge."

" They make a track to the water's edge——." And she said, " Over that bridge which shall be built with our bodies, who will pass ? "

He said, " *The entire human race.*"

And the woman grasped her staff.

And I saw her turn down that dark path to the river.

And I awoke ; and all about me was the yellow afternoon light : the sinking sun lit up the fingers of the milk bushes ; and my horse stood by me quietly feeding. And I turned on my side, and I watched the ants run by thousands in the red sand. I thought I would go on my way now—the afternoon was cooler. Then a drowsiness crept over me again, and I laid back my head and fell asleep.

And I dreamed a dream.

I dreamed I saw a land. And on the hills walked brave women and brave men, hand in hand. And they looked into each other's eyes, and they were not afraid.

And I saw the women also hold each other's hands.

And I said to him beside me, " What place is this ? "

And he said, " This is heaven."

And I said, "Where is it ? "

And he answered, " On earth."

And I said, " When shall these things be ? "

And he answered, " In the Future."

And I awoke, and all about me was the sunset light ; and on the low hills the sun lay, and a delicious coolness had crept over everything ; and the ants were going slowly home. And I walked

towards my horse, who stood quietly
feeding. Then the sun passed down
behind the hills; but I knew that the
next day he would arise again.

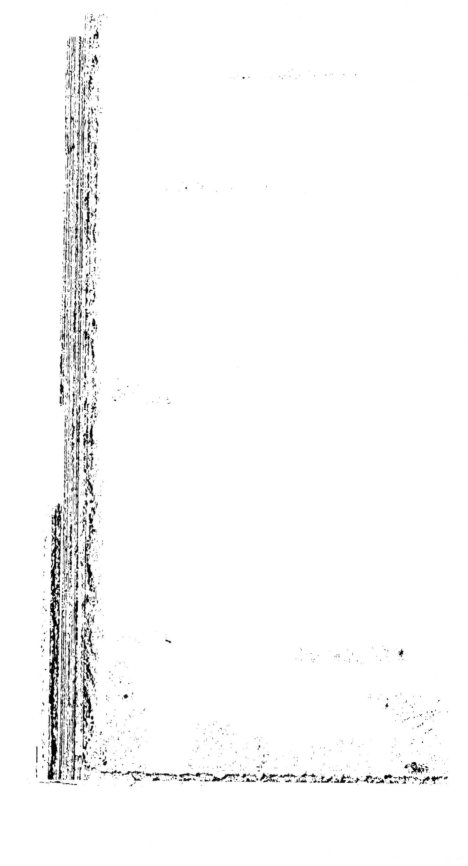

A DREAM OF WILD BEES.

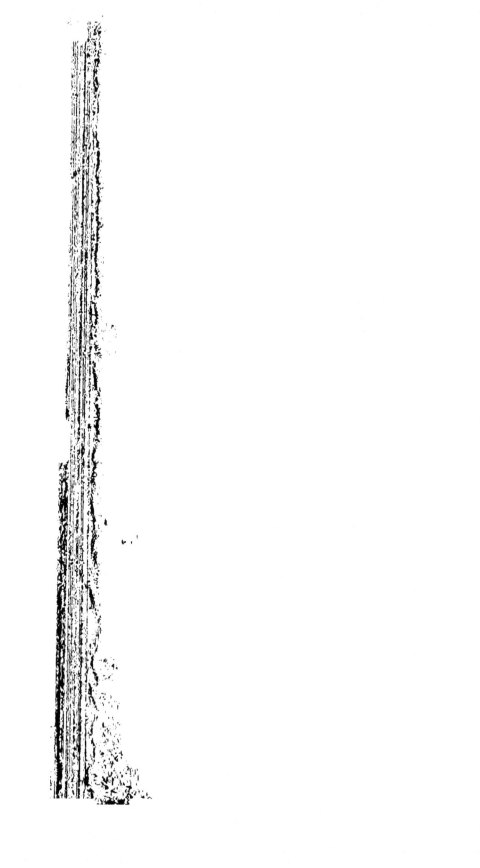

A DREAM OF WILD BEES.

MOTHER sat alone at an open window. Through it came the voices of the children as they played under the acacia-trees, and the breath of the hot afternoon air. In and out of the room flew the bees, the wild bees, with their legs yellow with pollen, going to and from the acacia-trees, droning all the while. She sat on a low chair before the table and darned. She took her work from the great basket that stood before her on the table: some lay on her knee and half covered the book that

rested there. She watched the needle go in and out; and the dreary hum of the bees and the noise of the children's voices became a confused murmur in her ears, as she worked slowly and more slowly. Then the bees, the long-legged wasp-like fellows who make no honey, flew closer and closer to her head, droning. Then she grew more and more drowsy, and she laid her hand, with the stocking over it, on the edge of the table, and leaned her head upon it. And the voices of the children outside grew more and more dreamy, came now far, now near; then she did not hear them, but she felt under her heart where the ninth child lay. Bent forward and sleeping there, with the bees flying about her head, she had a weird brain-picture; she thought the bees lengthened and lengthened themselves out and became human creatures and moved round

and round her. Then one came to her
softly, saying, "Let me lay my hand
upon thy side where the child sleeps.
If I shall touch him he shall be as I."

She asked, "Who are you?"

And he said, "I am Health. Whom
I touch will have always the red blood
dancing in his veins; he will not know
weariness nor pain; life will be a long
laugh to him."

"No," said another, "let me touch;
for I am Wealth. If I touch him
material care shall not feed on him.
He shall live on the blood and sinews
of his fellow-men, if he will; and what
his eye lusts for, his hand will have.
He shall not know 'I want.'" And the
child lay still like lead.

And another said, "Let me touch
him: I am Fame. The man I touch,
I lead to a high hill where all men may
see him When he dies he is not for-

gotten, his name rings down the cen-
turies, each echoes it on to his fellows.
Think—not to be forgotten through the
ages ! "

And the mother lay breathing steadily,
but in the brain-picture they pressed
closer to her.

" Let me touch the child," said one,
" for I am Love. If I touch him he
shall not walk through life alone. In
the greatest dark, when he puts out his
hand he shall find another hand by it.
When the world is against him, another
shall say, ' *You and I.*' " And the child
trembled.

But another pressed close and said,
" Let me touch; for I am Talent. I
can do all things—that have been done
before. I touch the soldier, the states-
man, the thinker, and the politician who
succeed; and the writer who is never
before his time, and never behind it. If

I touch the child he shall not weep for failure."

About the mother's head the bees were flying, touching her with their long tapering limbs ; and, in her brain-picture, out of the shadow of the room came one with sallow face, deep-lined, the cheeks drawn into hollows, and a mouth smiling quiveringly. He stretched out his hand. And the mother drew back, and cried, " Who are you ? " He answered nothing ; and she looked up between his eyelids. And she said, " What can you give the child—health ? " And he said, " The man I touch, there wakes up in his blood a burning fever, that shall lick his blood as fire. The fever that I will give him shall be cured when his life is cured."

" You give wealth ? "

He shook his head. " The man whom I touch, when he bends to pick up gold, he sees suddenly a light over his head in the sky; while he looks up to see it, the gold slips from between his fingers, or sometimes another passing takes it from them."

" Fame ? "

He answered, " Likely not. For the man I touch there is a path traced out in the sand by a finger which no man sees. That he must follow. Sometimes it leads almost to the top, and then turns down suddenly into the valley. He must follow it, though none else sees the tracing."

" Love ? "

He said, " He shall hunger for it— but he shall not find it. When he stretches out his arms to it, and would lay his heart against a thing he loves, then, far off along the horizon he shall see a light play. He must go towards it. The thing he loves will not journey with him; he must travel alone. When he presses somewhat to his burning heart, crying, ' Mine, mine, my own!' he shall hear a voice — ' Renounce! renounce! this is not thine!' "

" He shall succeed ? "

He said, " He shall fail. When he runs with others they shall reach the goal before him. For strange voices shall call to him and strange lights shall beckon him, and he must wait and listen. And this shall be the strangest : far off across the burning sands where, to other men, there is only the desert's waste, he shall see a blue sea! On that sea the sun shines always, and the water is blue as burning amethyst, and the foam is white on the shore. A great land rises from it, and he shall see upon the mountain-tops burning gold."

The mother said, " He shall reach it ? "

And he smiled curiously.

She said, " It is real ? "

And he said, " What *is* real ? "

And she looked up between his half-closed eyelids, and said, " Touch."

And he leaned forward and laid his hand upon the sleeper, and whispered to it, smiling ; and this only she heard— *" This shall be thy reward—that the ideal shall be real to thee."*

And the child trembled ; but the mother slept on heavily and her brain-picture vanished. But deep within her the antenatal thing that lay here had a dream. In those eyes that had never seen the day, in that half-shaped brain was a sensation of light ! Light—that it never had seen. Light—that perhaps it never should see. Light—that existed somewhere !

And already it had its reward : the Ideal was real to it.

London.

IN A RUINED CHAPEL.

[cannot] fo

IN A RUINED CHAPEL.

THERE are four bare walls; there is a Christ upon the walls, in red, carrying his cross; there is a Blessèd Bambino with the face rubbed out; there is Madonna in blue and red; there are Roman soldiers and a Christ with tied hands. All the roof is gone; overhead is the blue, blue Italian sky; the rain has beaten holes in the walls, and the plaster is peeling from it. The chapel stands here alone upon the promontory, and by day and by night the sea breaks at its feet. Some say that it

was set here by the monks from the
island down below, that they might
bring their sick here in times of deadly
plague. Some say that it was set here
that the passing monks and friars, as
they hurried by upon the roadway,
might stop and say their prayers here.
Now no one stops to pray here, and
the sick come no more to be healed.

Behind it runs the old Roman road.
If you climb it and come and sit there
alone on a hot sunny day you may
almost hear at last the clink of the
Roman soldiers upon the pavement, and
the sound of that older time, as you sit
there in the sun, when Hannibal and
his men broke through the brushwood,
and no road was.

Now it is very quiet. Sometimes a
peasant girl comes riding by betweer
her panniers, and you hear the mule's
feet beat upon the bricks of the pave-

ment ; sometimes an old woman goes past with a bundle of weeds upon her head, or a brigand-looking man hurries by with a bundle of sticks in his hand ; but for the rest the Chapel lies here alone upon the promontory, between the two bays and hears the sea break at its feet.

I came here one winter's day when the midday sun shone hot on the bricks of the Roman road. I was weary, and the way seemed steep. I walked into the chapel to the broken window, and looked out across the bay. Far off, across the blue, blue water, were towns and villages, hanging white and red dots, upon the mountain-sides, and the blue mountains rose up into the sky, and now stood out from it and now melted back again.

The mountains seemed calling to me,

but I knew there would never be a bridge built from them to me ; never, never, never ! I shaded my eyes with my hand and turned away. I could not bear to look at them.

I walked through the ruined Chapel, and looked at the Christ in red carrying his cross, and the Blessèd rubbed-out Bambino, and the Roman soldiers, and the folded hands, and the reed ; and I went and sat down in the open porch upon a stone. At my feet was the small bay, with its white row of houses buried among the olive trees ; the water broke in a long, thin, white line of foam along the shore ; and I leaned my elbows on my knees. I wás tired, very tired ; tired with a tiredness that seemed older than the heat of the day and the shining of the sun on the bricks of the Roman road ; and I lay my head upon my knees ; I heard the breaking of the water on the rocks three hundred feet below, and the rustling of the wind among the olive trees and the ruined arches, and then I fell asleep there. I had a dream.

A man cried up to God, and God sent down an angel to help him; and the angel came back and said, " I cannot help that man."

God said, " How is it with him ? "

And the angel said, " He cries out continually that one has injured him; and he would forgive him and he cannot."

God said, " What have you done for him ? "

The angel said, " All ——. I took him by the hand, and I said, ' See, when other men speak ill of that man do you speak well of him ; secretly, in ways he shall not know, serve him ; if you have anything you value share it with him, so, serving him, you will at last come to feel possession in him, and you will forgive.' And he said, ' I will do it.' Afterwards, as I passed by in the dark of night, I heard one crying out, ' I have done all. It helps nothing! My speaking well of him helps me nothing! If I share my heart's blood with him, is the burning within me less? I cannot forgive; I cannot forgive! Oh, God, I cannot forgive!'

" I said to him, ' See here, look back on all your past. See from your childhood all smallness, all indirectness that has been yours; look well at it, and in its light do you not see every man your brother? Are you so sinless you have right to hate?'

" He looked, and said, ' Yes, you are right; I too have failed, and I forgive my fellow. Go, I am satisfied; I have forgiven;' and he laid him down peacefully and folded his hands on his breast,

and I thought it was well with him.
But scarcely had my wings rustled
and I turned to come up here, when
I heard one crying out on earth again,
'I cannot forgive! I cannot forgive!
Oh, God, God, I cannot forgive! It
is better to die than to hate! I can-
not forgive! I cannot forgive!' And
I went and stood outside his door in
the dark, and I heard him cry, 'I have
not sinned so, not so! If I have torn
my fellows' flesh ever so little, I have
kneeled down and kissed the wound
with my mouth till it was healed. I
have not willed that any soul should
be lost through hate of me. If they
have but fancied that I wronged them
I have lain down on the ground before
them that they might tread on me, and
so, seeing my humiliation, forgive and
not be lost through hating me; they
have not cared that my soul should

be lost ; they have not willed to save
me ; they have not tried that I should
forgive them !'

"I said to him, 'See here, be thou
content ; do *not* forgive : forget this
soul and its injury ; go on your way.
In the next world perhaps——'

"He cried, 'Go from me, you under-
stand nothing ! What is the next world
to me ! I am lost now, to-day. I
cannot see the sunlight shine, the dust
is in my throat, the sand is in my eyes !
Go from me, you know nothing ! Oh,
once again before I die to see that the
world is beautiful ! Oh, God, God,
I cannot live and not love. I cannot
live and hate. Oh, God, God, God !'
So I left him crying out and came back
here."

God said, "This man's soul must be
saved."

And the angel said "How ?"

God said, "Go down you, and save it."

The angel said, "What more shall I do?"

Then God bent down and whispered in the angel's ear, and the angel spread out its wings and went down to earth.

And partly I woke, sitting there upon the broken stone with my head on my knee; but I was too weary to rise. I heard the wind roam through the olive trees and among the ruined arches, and then I slept again.

The angel went down and found the man with the bitter heart and took him by the hand, and led him to a certain spot.

Now the man wist not where it was the angel would take him nor what he would show him there. And when they came

the angel shaded the man's eyes with his
wing, and when he moved it the man
saw somewhat on the earth before them.
For God had given it to that angel to
unclothe a human soul; to take from it
all those outward attributes of form, and
colour, and age, and sex, whereby one
man is known from among his fellows
and is marked off from the rest, and
the soul lay before them, bare, as a man
turning his eye inwards beholds himself.

They saw its past, its childhood, the
tiny life with the dew upon it; they saw
its youth when the dew was melting,
and the creature raised its Lilliputian
mouth to drink from a cup too large for
it, and they saw how the water spilt;
they saw its hopes that were never
realized; they saw its hours of intel-
lectual blindness, men call sin; they
saw its hours of all-radiating insight,
which men call righteousness; they saw

its hour of strength, when it leaped to its feet crying, " I am omnipotent ; " its hour of weakness, when it fell to the earth and grasped dust only ; they saw what it might have been, but never would be.

The man bent forward.

And the angel said, " What is it ? "

He answered, "It is *I* ! it is myself ! " And he went forward as if he would have lain his heart against it ; but the angel held him back and covered his eyes.

Now God had given power to the angel further to unclothe that soul, to take from it all those outward attributes of time and place and circumstance whereby the individual life is marked off from the life of the whole.

Again the angel uncovered the man's eyes, and he looked. He saw before him that which in its tiny drop reflects the whole universe ; he saw that which marks within itself the step of the furthest star, and tells how the crystal grows under ground where no eye has seen it; that which is where the germ in the egg stirs; which moves the outstretched fingers of the little new-born babe, and keeps the leaves of the trees pointing upward; which moves where the jelly-fish sail alone on the sunny seas, and is where the lichens form on the mountains' rocks.

And the man looked.

And the angel touched him.

But the man bowed his head and shuddered. He whispered—"*It is God!*"

And the angel re-covered the man's eyes. And when he uncovered them there was one walking from them a little way off;—for the angel had re-clothed the soul in its outward form and vesture—and the man knew who it was.

And the angel said, " Do you know him ? "

And the man said, "I know him," and he looked after the figure.

And the angel said, "Have you forgiven him?"

But the man said, "*How beautiful my brother is!*"

And the angel looked into the man's eyes, and he shaded his own face with his wing from the light. He laughed softly and went up to God.

But the men were together on earth.

I awoke.

The blue, blue sky was over my head, and the waves were breaking below on the shore. I walked through the little chapel, and I saw the Madonna in blue and red, and the Christ carrying his cross, and the Roman soldiers with the rod, and the Blessèd Bambino with its broken face; and then I walked down the sloping rock to the brick pathway.

The olive trees stood up on either side of the road, their black berries and pale-green leaves stood out against the sky; and the little ice-plants hung from the crevices in the stone wall. It seemed to me as if it must have rained while I was asleep. I thought I had never seen the heavens and the earth look so beautiful before. I walked down the road. The old, old, old tiredness was gone.

Presently there came a peasant boy down the path leading his ass; she had two large panniers fastened to her sides; and they went down the road before me.

I had never seen him before; but I should have liked to walk by him and to have held his hand——only, he would not have known why.

Alassio, Italy.

LIFE'S GIFTS.

LIFE'S GIFTS.

 SAW a woman sleeping. In her sleep she dreamt Life stood before her, and held in each hand a gift—in the one Love, in the other Freedom. And she said to the woman, " Choose ! "

And the woman waited long : and she said, " Freedom ! "

And Life said, " Thou hast well chosen. If thou hadst said, ' Love,' I would have given thee that thou didst ask for ; and I would have gone from thee, and returned to thee no more. Now, the day will come when I shall

return.   In that day I shall bear both
gifts in one hand."

I heard the woman laugh in her sleep.

London.

THE ARTIST'S SECRET.

THE ARTIST'S SECRET.

HERE was an artist once, and he painted a picture. Other artists had colours richer and rarer, and painted more notable pictures. He painted his with one colour, there was a wonderful red glow on it; and the people went up and down, saying, "We like the picture, we like the glow."

The other artists came and said, "Where does he get his colour from?" They asked him; and he smiled and said, "I cannot tell you"; and worked on with his head bent low.

And one went to the far East and bought costly pigments, and made a rare colour and painted, but after a time the picture faded. Another read in the old books, and made a colour rich and rare, but when he had put it on the picture it was dead.

But the artist painted on. Always the work got redder and redder, and the artist grew whiter and whiter. At last one day they found him dead before his picture, and they took him up to bury him. The other men looked about in all the pots and crucibles, but they found nothing they had not.

And when they undressed him to put his grave-clothes on him, they found above his left breast the mark of a wound—it was an old, old wound, that must have been there all his life, for the edges were old and hardened; but Death, who seals all things, had drawn the edges together, and closed it up.

And they buried him. And still the people went about saying, " Where did he find his colour from ? "

And it came to pass that after a while the artist was forgotten—but the work lived.

St. Leonards-on-Sea.

"*I THOUGHT I STOOD.*"

"*I THOUGHT I STOOD.*"

I.

 THOUGHT I stood in Heaven before God's throne, and God asked me what I had come for. I said I had come to arraign my brother, Man.

God said, "What has he done?"

I said, "He has taken my sister, Woman, and has stricken her, and wounded her, and thrust her out into the streets; she lies there prostrate. His hands are red with blood. *I* am here to arraign him; that the kingdom be taken from him, because he is not worthy, and given unto me. My hands are pure."

I showed them. '

God said, "Thy hands are pure.— Lift up thy robe."

I raised it; my feet were red, blood-red, as if I had trodden in wine.

God said, "How is this?"

I said, "Dear Lord, the streets on earth are full of mire. If I should walk straight on in them my outer robe might be bespotted, you see how white it is! Therefore I pick my way."

God said, "*On what?*"

I was silent, and I let my robe fall. I wrapped my mantle about my head. I went out softly. I was afraid that the angels would see me.

II.

Once more I stood at the gate of Heaven, I and another. We held fast by one another; we were very tired. We looked up at the great gates; the angels opened them, and we went in. The mud was on our garments. We walked across the marble floor, and up to the great throne. Then the angels divided us. Her, they set upon the top step, but me, upon the bottom; for, they said, " Last time this woman came here she left red foot-marks on the floor; we had to wash them out with our tears. Let her not go up."

Then she, with whom I came, looked back, and stretched out her hand to me; and I went and stood beside her. And the angels, they, the shining ones who never sinned and never suffered, walked by us to and fro and up and down; I think we should have felt a little lonely there if it had not been for one another, the angels were so bright.

God asked me what I had come for;

and I drew my sister forward a little that he might see her.

God said, " How is it you are here together to-day ? "

I said, " She was upon the ground in the street, and they passed over her ; I lay down by her, and she put her arms around my neck, and so I lifted her, and we two rose together."

God said, " Whom are you now come to accuse before me ? "

I said, " We are come to accuse no man."

And God bent, and said, " My children—what is it that ye seek ? "

And she beside me drew my hand that I should speak for both.

I said, " We have come to ask that thou shouldst speak to Man, our brother, and give us a message for him that he might understand, and that he might—— "

God said, "Go, take the message down to him!"

I said, "But what *is* the message?"

God said, "Upon your hearts it is written; take it down to him."

And we turned to go; the angels went with us to the door. They looked at us.

And one said—"Ai! but their dresses are beautiful!"

And the other said, "I thought it was mire when they came in, but see, it is all golden!"

But another said, "Hush, it is the light from their faces!"

And we went down to him.

Alassio, Italy.

*THE SUNLIGHT LAY ACROSS MY
BED.*

THE SUNLIGHT LAY ACROSS MY BED,——

IN the dark one night I lay upon my bed. I heard the policeman's feet beat on the pavement ; I heard the wheels of carriages roll home from houses of entertainment ; I heard a woman's laugh below my window—— and then I fell asleep. And in the dark I dreamt a dream. I dreamt God took my soul to Hell.

Hell was a fair place ; the water of the lake was blue.

I said to God, " I like this place."

God said, "Ay, dost thou!"

Birds sang, turf came to the water-edge, and trees grew from it. Away off among the trees I saw beautiful women walking. Their clothes were of many delicate colours and clung to them, and they were tall and graceful and had yellow hair. Their robes trailed over the grass. They glided in and out among the trees, and over their heads hung yellow fruit like large pears of melted gold.

I said, " It is very fair; I would go up and taste the——"

God said, " Wait."

And after a while I noticed a very fair woman pass: she looked this way and that, and drew down a branch, and it seemed she kissed the fruit upon it softly, and went on her way, and her dress made no rustle as she passed over the grass. And when I saw her no more, from among the stems came another woman fair as she had been, in a delicate tinted robe ; she looked this way and that. When she saw no one there she drew down the fruit, and when she had looked over it to find a place, she put her mouth to it softly, and went away. And I saw other and other women come, making no noise, and they glided away also over the grass.

And I said to God, "What are they doing ? "

God said, " They are poisoning."

And I said, " How ? "

God said, " They touch it with their lips, when they have made a tiny wound in it with their fore-teeth they set in it that which is under their tongues : they close it with their lip—that no man may see the place, and pass on."

I said to God, " Why do they do it ? "

God said, " That another may not eat."

I said to God, " But if they poison all then none dare eat ; what do they gain ? "

God said, " Nothing."

I said, " Are they not afraid they themselves may bite where another has bitten ? "

God said, " They are afraid. In Hell all men fear."

He called me further. And the water of the lake seemed less blue.

Then, to the right among the trees were men working. And I said to God, " I should like to go and work with them. Hell must be a very fruitful place, the grass is so green."

God said, " Nothing grows in the garden they are making."

We stood looking ; and I saw them working among the bushes, digging holes, but in them they set nothing ; and when they had covered

them with sticks and earth each went
a way off and sat behind the bushes
watching; and I noticed that as each
walked he set his foot down carefully
looking where he trod. I said to God,
" What are they doing ? "

God said, " Making pitfalls into which
their fellows may sink."

I said to God, " Why do they do
it ? "

God said, " Because each thinks that
when his brother falls he will rise."

I said to God, " How will he rise ? "

God said, " He will not rise."

And I saw their eyes gleam from
behind the bushes.

I said to God, "Are these men sane?"

God said, " They are not sane ; there
is no sane man in Hell."

And he told me to come further.

And I looked where I trod.

And we came where Hell opened

into a plain, and a great house stood
there.   Marble pillars upheld the roof,
and white marble steps led up to it.
The wind of heaven blew through it.
Only at the back hung a thick curtain.
Fair men and women there feasted at
long tables.   They danced, and I saw
the robes of women flutter in the air
and heard the laugh of strong men.
What they feasted with was wine; they
drew it from large jars which stood
somewhat in the background, and I
saw the wine sparkle as they drew it.

And I said to God, " I should like to go
up and drink."   And God said, "Wait."
And I saw men coming in to the Banquet
House; they came in from the back
and lifted the corner of the curtain
at the sides and crept in quickly; and
they let the curtain fall behind them ;
they bore great jars they could
hardly carry.   And the men and women

crowded round them, and the new-
comers opened their jars and gave them
of the wine to drink; and I saw that
the women drank even more greedily
than the men. And when others had
well drunken they set the jars among
the old ones beside the wall, and took
their places at the table. And I saw
that some of the jars were very old and
mildewed and dusty, but others had still
drops of new must on them and shone
from the furnace.

And I said to God, "What is that?"
For amid the sound of the singing, and
over the dancing of feet, and over the
laughing across the wine-cups I heard
a cry.

And God said, "Stand a way off."

And he took me where I saw both
sides of the curtain. Behind the house
was the wine-press where the wine was
made I saw the grapes crushed, and

· I heard them cry. I said, " Do not they on the other side hear it ? "

God said, " The curtain is thick ; they are feasting."

And I said, " But the men who came in last. They saw ? "

God said, " They let the curtain fall behind them—and they forget ! "

I said, " How came they by their jars of wine ? "

God said, " In the treading of the press these are they who came to the top ; they have climbed out over the edge, and filled their jars from below, and have gone into the house."

And I said, " And if they had fallen as they climbed—— ? "

God said, " They had been wine."

I stood a way off watching in the sunshine, and I shivered.

God lay in the sunshine watching too.

Then there rose one among the

feasters, who said, " My brethren, let us pray ! "

And all the men and women rose · and strong men bowed their heads, and mothers folded their little children's hands together, and turned their faces upwards, to the roof. And he who first had risen stood at the table head, and stretched out both his hands, and his beard was long and white, and his sleeves and his beard had been dipped in wine ; and because the sleeves were wide and full they held much wine, and it dropped down upon the floor.

And he cried, " My brothers and my sisters, let us pray."

And all the men and women answered, " Let us pray."

He cried, " For this fair banquet-house we thank thee, Lord."

And all the men and women said " We thank thee, Lord."

" Thine is this house, dear Lord."

" Thine is this house."

" For us hast thou made it."

" For us."

" Oh, fill our jars with wine, dear Lord."

" Our jars with wine."

" Give peace and plenty in our time, dear Lord."

" Peace and plenty in our time "——
I said to God, " Whom is it they are talking to ? "   God said, " Do *I* know whom they speak of ? "   And I saw they were looking up at the roof; but out in the sunshine, God lay.

" ——dear Lord ! "

" Dear Lord."

" Our children's children, Lord, shall rise and call thee blessed."

" Our children's children, Lord."——
I said to God, " The grapes are crying ! " God said, "Still ! *I* hear. them "——
" shall call thee blessed."

" Shall call thee blessed."

" Pour forth more wine upon us, Lord."

" More wine."

" More wine."

" More wine ! "

" Wine ! ! "

" Wine ! ! "

" Wine ! ! ! "

" Dear Lord ! "

Then men and women sat down and the feast went on. And mothers poured out wine and fed their little children with it, and men held up the cup to women's lips and cried, " Beloved ! drink," and women filled their lovers' flagons and held them up ; and yet the feast went on.

And after a while I looked, and I saw the curtain that hung behind the house moving.

I said to God, " Is it a wind ? "

God said, " A wind."

And it seemed to me, that against the curtain I saw pressed the forms of men and women. And after a while the feasters saw it move, and they whispered, one to another. Then some rose and gathered the most worn-out cups. and into them they put what was left at the bottom of other vessels. Mothers whispered to their children, " Do not drink all, save a little drop when you have drunk " And when they had collected all the dregs they slipped the cups out under the bottom of the curtain without lifting it. After a while the curtain left off moving.

I said to God, " How is it so quiet ?"

He said, " They have gone away to drink it."

I said, " *They* drink it—*their own !*"

God said, " It comes from this side of the curtain, and they are very thirsty."

Then the feast went on, and after a while I saw a small, white hand slipped in below the curtain's edge along the floor; and it motioned towards the wine jars.

And I said to God, " Why is that hand so bloodless ? "

And God said, " It is a wine-pressed hand."

And men saw it and started to their feet ; and women cried. and ran to the great wine jars, and threw their arms around them, and cried, " Ours, our own, our beloved !" and twined their long hair about them.

I said to God, " Why are they frightened of that one small hand ?"

God answered, " Because it is so white."

And men ran in a great company towards the curtain, and struggled there. I heard them strike upon the floor. And when they moved away the curtain hung smooth and still; and there was a small stain upon the floor.

I said to God, "Why do they not wash it out?"

God said, "They cannot."

And they took small stones and put them down along the edge of the curtain to keep it down. Then the men and women sat down again at the tables.

And I said to God, "Will those stones keep it down?"

God said, "What think you?"

I said, "If the wind blew——"

God said, "If the wind blew?"

And the feast went on.

And suddenly I cried to God, "If one should rise among them, even of themselves, and start up from the table and should cast away his cup, and cry, 'My brothers and my sisters, stay! what is it that we drink?'——and with his sword should cut in two the curtain, and holding wide the fragments, cry, 'Brothers, sisters, see! it is not wine, not wine! not wine! My brothers, oh, my sisters—!' and he should overturn the——"

God said, " Be still !——, see there."

I looked : before the banquet-house, among the grass, I saw a row of mounds, flowers covered them, and gilded marble stood at their heads. I asked God what they were.

He answered, " They are the graves of those who rose up at the feast and cried."

And I asked God how they came there.

He said, " The men of the banquet-house rose and cast them down backwards."

I said, " Who buried them ? "

God said, " The men who cast them down."

I said, " How came it that they threw them down, and then set marble over them ? "

God said, " Because the bones cried out, they covered them."

And among the grass and weeds I saw an unburied body lying ; and I asked God why it was.

God said, " Because it was thrown down only yesterday. In a little while, when the flesh shall have fallen from its bones, they will bury it also, and plant flowers over it."

And still the feast went on.

Men and women sat at the tables quaffing great bowls. Some rose, and threw their arms about each other, and danced and sang. They pledged each other in the wine, and kissed each other's blood-red lips.

Higher and higher grew the revels.

Men, when they had drunk till they

could no longer, threw what was left in their glasses up to the roof, and let it fall back in cascades. Women dyed their children's garments in the wine, and fed them on it till their tiny mouths were red. Sometimes, as the dancers whirled, they overturned a vessel, and their garments were bespattered. Children sat upon the floor with great bowls of wine, and swam rose-leaves on it, for boats. They put their hands in the wine and blew large red bubbles.

And higher and higher grew the revels, and wilder the dancing, and louder and louder the singing. But here and there among the revellers were those who did not revel. I saw that at the tables here and there were men who sat with their elbows on the board and hands shading their eyes; they looked into the wine-cup beneath them, and did not drink. And when one touched them lightly on the shoulder, bidding them to rise and dance and sing, they started, and then looked down, and sat there watching the wine in the cup, but they did not move.

And here and there I saw a woman sit apart. The others danced and sang and fed their children, but she sat silent with her head aside as though she listened. Her little children plucked her gown; she did not see them; she was listening to some sound, but she did not stir.

The revels grew higher. Men drank till they could drink no longer, and lay their heads upon the table sleeping heavily. Women who could dance no more leaned back on the benches with their heads against their lovers' shoulders. Little children, sick with wine, lay down upon the edges of their mothers' robes.

Sometimes, a man rose suddenly, and as he staggered struck the tables and overthrew the benches; some leaned upon the balustrades sick unto death. Here and there one rose who staggered to the wine jars and lay down beside them. He turned the wine tap, but sleep overcame him as he lay there, and the wine ran out.

Slowly the thin, red stream ran across the white marbled floor; it reached the stone steps; slowly, slowly, slowly it trickled down, from step to step, from step to step: then it sank into the earth. A thin white smoke rose up from it.

I was silent; I could not breathe; but God called me to come further.

And after I had travelled for a while I came where on seven hills lay the ruins of a mighty banquet-house larger and stronger than the one which I had seen standing.

I said to God, "What did the men
,who built it here?"

God said, "They feasted."

I said, "On what?"

God said, "On wine."

And I looked; and it seemed to me
that behind the ruins lay still a large
circular hollow within the earth where
a foot of the wine-press had stood.

I said to God, "How came it that
this large house fell?"

God said, "Because the earth was
sodden."

He called me to come further.

And at last we came upon a hill
where blue waters played, and white
marble lay upon the earth. I said to
God, "What was here once?"

God said, "A pleasure house."

I looked, and at my feet great pillars
lay. I cried aloud for joy to God,
"The marble blossoms!"

God said, " Ay, 'twas a fairy house. There has not been one like to it, nor ever shall be. The pillars and the porticoes blossomed; and the wine cups were as gathered flowers : on this side all the curtain was broidered with fair designs, the stitching was of gold."

I said to God, " How came it that it fell ? "

God said, " On the side of the winepress it was dark."

And as we travelled, we came where lay a mighty ridge of sand, and a dark river ran there ; and there rose two vast mounds.

I said to God, " They are very mighty."

God said, " Ay, exceeding great."

And I listened.

God asked me what I was listening to.

And I said, " A sound of weeping, and I hear the sound of strokes, but I cannot tell whence it comes."

God said, "It is the echo of the wine-press lingering still among the coping-stones upon the mounds. A banquet-house stood here."

And he called me to come further.

Upon a barren hill-side, where the soil was arid, God called me to stand still. And I looked around.

God said, "There was a feasting-house here once upon a time."

I said to God, "I see no mark of any!"

God said, "There was not left one stone upon another that has not been thrown down." And I looked round; and on the hill-side was a lonely grave.

I said to God, "What lies there?"

He said, "A vine truss, bruised in the wine-press!"

And at the head of the grave stood a cross, and on its foot lay a crown of thorns.

And as I turned to go, I looked backward. The wine-press and the banquet-house were gone ; but the grave yet stood.

And when I came to the edge of a long ridge there opened out before me a wide plain of sand. And when I looked downward I saw great stones lie shattered ; and the desert sand had half covered them over.

I said to God, " There is writing on them, but I cannot read it."

And God blew aside the desert sand, and I read the writing : " Weighed in the balance, and found——" but the last word was wanting.

And I said to God, " It was a banquet-house ? "

God said, " Ay, a banquet-house."

I said, "There was a wine-press here?"

God said, " There was a wine-press."

I asked no further question. I was

very weary; I shaded my eyes with my hand, and looked through the pink evening light.

Far off, across the sand, I saw two figures standing. With wings upfolded high above their heads, and stern faces set, neither man nor beast, they looked out across the desert sand, watching, watching, watching! I did not ask God what they were, for I knew what the answer would be.

And, further and yet further, in the evening light, I looked with my shaded eyes.

Far off, where the sands were thick and heavy, I saw a solitary pillar standing: the crown had fallen, and the sand had buried it. On the broken pillar sat a grey owl-of-the-desert, with folded wings; and in the evening light I saw the desert fox creep past it, trailing his brush across the sand.

Further, yet further, as I looked across the desert, I saw the sand gathered into heaps as though it covered something.

I cried to God, "Oh, I am so weary."

God said, "You have seen only one half of Hell."

I said, "I cannot see more, I am afraid of Hell. In my own narrow little path I dare not walk because I think that one has dug a pitfall for me; and if I put my hand to take a fruit I draw it back again because I think it has been kissed already. If I look out across the plains, the mounds are burial heaps; and when I pass among the stones I hear them crying aloud. When I see men dancing I hear the time beaten in with sobs; and their wine is living! Oh, I cannot bear Hell!"

God said, "Where will you go?"

I said " To the earth from which I came ; it was better there."

And God laughed at me ; and I wondered why he laughed.

God said, " Come, and I will show you Heaven."

*   *   ⚹   ▪   ❋   ▪

And partly I awoke. It was still and dark ; the sound of the carriages had died in the street ; the woman who laughed was gone ; and the policeman's tread was heard no more. In the dark it seemed as if a great hand lay upon my heart, and crushed it. I tried to breathe and tossed from side to side ; and then again I fell asleep, and dreamed.

God took me to the edge of that world. It ended. I looked down. The gulf, it seemed to me, was fathomless ; and then I saw two bridges crossing it that both sloped upwards.

I said to God, " Is there no other way by which men cross it ? "

God said, " One ; it rises far from here and slopes straight upwards.

I asked God what the bridges' names were.

God said, " What matter for the names ? Call them the Good, the True, the Beautiful, if you will—you will yet not understand them."

I asked God how it was I could not see the third.

God said, " It is seen only by those who climb it."

I said, " Do they all lead to one heaven ? "

God said, " All Heaven is one · nevertheless some parts are higher than others ; those who reach the higher may always go down to rest in the lower ; but those in the lower may not have strength to climb to the higher; nevertheless the light is all one."

And I saw over the bridge nearest me, which was wider than the other, countless footmarks go. I asked God why so many went over it.

God said, " It slopes less deeply, and leads to the first heaven."

And I saw that some of the footmarks were of feet returning. I asked God how it was.

He said, " No man who has once entered Heaven ever leaves it; but some, when they have gone half way, turn back, because they are afraid there is no land beyond."

I said, " Has none ever returned ? "

God said, " No ; once in Heaven always in Heaven."

And God took me over. And when we came to one of the great doors—for Heaven has more doors than one, and they are all open—the posts rose up so high on either side I could not see the top, nor indeed if there were any.

And it seemed to me so wide that all Hell could go in through it.

I said to God, "Which is the larger, Heaven or Hell?"

God said, "Hell is as widé, but Heaven is deeper. All Hell could be engulfed in Heaven, but all Heaven could not be engulfed in Hell."

And we entered. It was a still great land. The mountains rose on every hand, and there was a pale clear light; and I saw it came from the rocks and stones. I asked God how it was.

But God did not answer me.

I looked and wondered, for I had thought Heaven would be otherwise. And after a while it began to grow brighter, as if the day were breaking, and I asked God if the sun were not going to rise.

God said, "No; we are coming to where the people are."

And as we went on it grew brighter and brighter till it was burning day; and on the rock were flowers blooming, and trees blossomed at the roadside; and streams of water ran everywhere, and I heard the birds singing; I asked God where they were.

God said, "It is the people calling to one another."

And when we came nearer I saw them walking, and they shone as they walked. I asked God how it was they wore no covering.

God said, "Because all their body gives the light; they dare not cover any part."

And I asked God what they were doing.

God said, "Shining on the plants that they may grow."

And I saw that some were working in companies, and some alone, but most were in twos, sometimes two men and sometimes two women ; but generally there was one man and one woman ; and I asked God how it was.

God said, "When one man and one woman shine together, it makes the most perfect light. Many plants need that for their growing. Nevertheless, there are more kinds of plants in Heaven than one, and they need many kinds of light."

And one from among the people came running towards me ; and when he came near it seemed to me that he and I had played together when we were little children, and that we had been born on the same day. And I told God what I felt ; God said, " All men feel so in

Heaven when another comes towards them."

And he who ran towards me held my hand, and led me through the bright lights. And when we came among the trees he sang aloud, and his companion answered, and it was a woman, and he showed me to her. She said, "He must have water"; and she took some in her hands, and fed me (I had been afraid to drink of the water in Hell), and they gathered fruit for me, and gave it me to eat. They said, "We shone long to make it ripen," and they laughed together as they saw me eat it.

The man said, "He is very weary; he must sleep" (for I had not dared to sleep in Hell), and he laid my head on his companion's knee and spread her hair out over me. I slept, and all the while in my sleep I thought I heard the birds calling across me　And when

I woke it was like early morning, with the dew on everything.

And the man took my hand and led me to a hidden spot among the rocks. The ground was very hard, but out of it were sprouting tiny plants, and there was a little stream running. He said, " This is a garden we are making, no one else knows of it. We shine here every day ; see, the ground has cracked with our shining, and this little stream is bursting out. See, the flowers are growing."

And he climbed on the rocks and picked from above two little flowers with dew on them, and gave them to me. And I took one in each hand ; my hands shone as I held them He said, " This garden is for all when it is finished." And he went away to his companion, and I went out into the great pathway.

And as I walked in the light I heard a loud sound of much singing. And when I came nearer I saw one with closed eyes, singing, and his fellows were standing round him ; and the light on the closed eyes was brighter than anything I had seen in Heaven. I asked one who it was. And he said, " Hush ! Our singing bird."

And I asked why the eyes shone so.

And he said, " They cannot see, and we have kissed them till they shone so."

And the people gathered closer round him.

And when I went a little further I saw a crowd crossing among the trees of light with great laughter. When they came close I saw they carried one without hands or feet. And a light came from the maimed limbs so bright that I could not look at them.

And I said to one, " What is it ? "

He answered, " This is our brother who once fell and lost his hands and feet, and since then he cannot help himself ; but we have touched the maimed stumps so often that now they shine brighter than anything in Heaven. We pass him on that he may shine on things that need much heat. No one is allowed to keep him long, he belongs to all " ; and they went on among the trees.

I said to God, " This is a strange land. I had thought blindness and maimedness were great evils. Here men make them to a rejoicing."

" God said, " Didst thou then think that love had *need* of eyes and hands ! "

And I walked down the shining way with palms on either hand. I said to God, " Ever since I was a little child and sat alone and cried, I have dreamed of this land, and now I will not go away again. I will stay here and shine." And I began to take off my garments, that I might shine as others in that land; but when I looked down I saw my body gave no light. I said to God, "How is it?"

God said, "Is there no dark blood in your heart; is it bitter against none?"

And I said, "Yes——"; and I thought—"Now is the time when I will tell God, that which I have been, meaning to tell him all along, how badly my fellow-men have treated me. How they have misunderstood me. How I have intended to be magnanimous and generous to them, and they ——." And I began to tell God; but when I looked down all the flowers were withering under my breath, and I was silent.

And God called me to come up higher, and I gathered my mantle about me and followed him.

And the rocks grew higher and steeper on every side; and we came at last to a place where a great mountain rose, whose top was lost in the clouds. And on its side I saw men working; and they picked at the earth with huge picks; and I saw that they laboured mightily. And some laboured in companies, but most laboured singly. And I saw the drops of sweat fall from their foreheads, and the muscles of their arms stand out with labour And I said, "I had not thought in heaven to see men labour so!" And I thought of the garden where men sang and loved, and I wondered that any should choose to labour on that bare mountain-side. And I saw upon the foreheads of the men as they worked a light, and the drops which fell from them as they worked had light.

And I asked God what they were seeking for.

And God touched my eyes, and I saw that what they found were small stones, which had been too bright for me to see before; and I saw that the light of the stones and the light on the men's foreheads was the same. And I saw that when one found a stone he passed it on to his fellow, and he to another, and he to another. No man kept the stone he found. And at times they gathered in great company about when a large stone was found, and raised a great shout so that the sky rang; then they worked on again.

And I asked God what they did with the stones they found at last. Then God touched my eyes again to make them stronger; and I looked, and at my very feet was a mighty crown. The light streamed out from it.

God said, " Each stone as they find it is set here."

And the crown was wrought according to a marvellous pattern; one pattern ran through all, yet each part was different.

I said to God, " How does each man know where to set his stone, so that the pattern is worked out ? "

God said, " Because in the light his forehead sheds each man sees faintly outlined that full crown."

And I said, " But how is it that each stone is joined along its edges to its fellows, so that there is no seam anywhere ? "

God said, " The stones are alive; they grow."

And I said, " But what does each man gain by his working ? "

God says, "He sees his outline filled."

I said, "But those stones which are last set cover those which were first; and those will again be covered by those which come later."

God said, "They are covered, but not hid. The light is the light of all. Without the first, no last."

And I said to God, "When will this crown be ended?"

And God said, "Look up!"

I looked up; and I saw the mountain tower above me, but its summit I could not see; it was lost in the clouds.

God said no more.

And I looked at the crown: then a longing seized me. Like the passion of a mother for the child whom death has taken; like the yearning of a friend for the friend whom life has buried; like the hunger of dying eyes for a life that is slipping; like the thirst of a soul for love at its first spring waking, so, but fiercer was the longing in me.

I cried to God, "I too will work here; I too will set stones in the wonderful pattern ; it shall grow beneath *my* hand. And if it be that, labouring here for years, I should not find one stone, at least I will be with the men that labour here. I shall hear their shout of joy when each stone is found ; I shall join in their triumph I shall shout among them ; I shall see the crown grow." So great was my longing as I looked at the crown, I thought a faint light fell from my forehead also.

God said, "Do you not hear the singing in the gardens ?"

I said, "No, I hear nothing ; I see only the crown." And I was dumb with longing ; I forgot all the flowers of the lower Heaven and the singing there. And I ran forward, and threw my mantle on the earth and bent to seize one of the mighty tools which lay there. I could not lift it from the earth.

God said, "Where hast *thou* earned the strength to raise it? Take up thy mantle."

And I took up my mantle and followed where God called me; but I looked back, and I saw the crown burning, my crown that I had loved.

Higher and higher we climbed, and the air grew thinner. Not a tree or plant was on the bare rocks, and the stillness was unbroken. My breath came hard and quick, and the blood crept within my finger-tips. I said to God, " Is this Heaven ?"

God said, "Yes ; it is the highest."

And still we climbed. I said to God, "I cannot breathe so high."

God said, " Because the air is pure ?"

And my head grew dizzy, and as I

climbed the blood burst from my finger-tips.

Then we came out upon **a** lonely mountain-top.

No living being moved there; but far off on a solitary peak I saw a lonely figure standing. Whether it were man or woman I could not tell; for partly it seemed the figure of a woman, but its limbs were the mighty limbs of a man. I asked God whether it was man or woman.

God said, " In the least Heaven sex reigns supreme ; in the higher it is not noticed; but in the highest it does not exist."

And I saw the figure bend over its work, and labour mightily, but what it laboured at I could not see.

I said to God, " How came it here ? "

God said, " By a bloody stair. Step by step it mounted from the lowest Hell, and day by day as Hell grew farther and Heaven no nearer, it hung alone between two worlds.   Hour by hour in that bitter struggle its limbs grew larger, till there fell from it rag by rag the garments which it started with.   Drops fell from its eyes as it strained them ; each step it climbed was wet with blood. Then it came out here."

And I thought of the garden where men sang with their arms around one another; and the mountain-side where they worked in company.   And I shuddered.

And I said, " Is it not terribly alone here ? "

God said, " It is never alone ! "

I said, " What has it for all its labour ? I see nothing return to it."

Then God touched my eyes, and I saw stretched out beneath us the plains of Heaven and Hell, and all that was within them.

God said, " From that lone height on which he stands, all things are open. To him is clear the shining in the garden, he sees the flower break forth and the streams sparkle ; no shout is raised upon the mountain-side but his ear may hear it. He sees the crown grow and the light shoot from it. All Hell is open to him. He sees the paths mount upwards. To him, Hell is the seed ground from which Heaven springs. He sees the sap ascending."

And I saw the figure bend over its work, and the light from its face fell upon it.

And I said to God, " What is it making ? "

And God said, " Music ! "

And he touched my ears, and I heard it.

And after a long while I whispered to God, " This is Heaven."

And God asked me why I was crying. But I could not answer for joy.

And the face turned from its work, and the light fell upon me. Then it grew so bright I could not see things separately ; and which were God, or the man, or I, I could not tell ; we were all blended. I cried to God, " Where are you ? " but there was no answer, only music and light.

Afterwards, when it had grown so dark again that I could see things separately, I found that I was standing there wrapped tight in my little old, brown, earthly cloak, and God and the man were separated from each other, and from me.

I did not dare say I would go and make music beside the man. I knew I could not reach even to his knee, nor move the instrument he played. But I thought I would stand there on my

little peak and sing an accompaniment
to that great music. And I tried; but
my voice failed. It piped and qua-
vered. I could not sing that tune. I
was silent.

Then God pointed to me, that I
should go out of Heaven.

And I cried to God, "Oh, let me
stay here! If indeed it be, as I know
it is, that I am not great enough to sing
upon the mountain, nor strong enough to
labour on its side, nor bright enough to
shine and love within the garden, at
least let me go down to the great
gateway; humbly I will kneel there
sweeping; and, as the saved pass in,
I will see the light upon their faces.
I shall hear the singing in the garden,
and the shout upon the hillside——"

God said, "It may not be;" he
pointed.

And I cried, "If I may not stay in

Heaven, then let me go down to Hell, and I will grasp the hands of men and women there; and slowly, holding one another's hands, we will work our way upwards."

Still God pointed.

And I threw myself upon the earth and cried, " Earth is so small, so mean! It is not meet a soul should see Heaven and be cast out again!"

And God laid his hand on me, and said, " Go back to earth: *that which you seek is there.*"

I awoke: it was morning. The silence and darkness of the night were gone. Through my narrow attic window I saw the light of another day. I closed my eyes and turned towards the wall: I could not look upon the dull grey world.

In the streets below, men and women streamed past by hundreds; I heard the beat **of** their feet on the pavement. Men on their way to business; servants on errands; boys hurrying to school; weary professors pacing slowly the old street; prostitutes, men and women, dragging their feet wearily after last night's debauch; artists with quick, impatient footsteps; tradesmen for orders; children to seek for bread. I heard the stream beat by. And at the alley's mouth, at the street corner, a broken barrel-organ was playing; sometimes **it** quavered and almost stopped, then went on again, like a broken human voice.

I listened: my heart scarcely moved; it was as cold as lead I could not bear the long day before me; and I tried **to** sleep again; yet still I heard the feet upon the pavement. And suddenly I heard them cry loud as they beat, " We are seeking!--we are seeking!

—we are seeking!" and the broken barrel-organ at the street corner sobbed, "The Beautiful!—the Beautiful!—the Beautiful!" And my heart, which had been dead, cried out with every throb, "Love!—Truth!—the Beautiful!—the Beautiful!" It was the music I had heard in Heaven that I could not sing there.

And fully I awoke.

Upon the faded quilt, across my bed a long yellow streak of pale London sunlight was lying. It fell through my narrow attic window.

I laughed. I rose.

I was glad the long day was before me.

Paris and London.

The Story of an African Farm. A Novel. By RALPH IRON (OLIVE SCHREINER). Price, 60 cents.

Glorinda. A Story. By ANNA BOWMAN DODD, author of "Cathedral Days." Price, 75 cents.

Casimir Maremma. A Story. By SIR ARTHUR HELPS, author of "Friends in Council," "The Story of Realmah," etc. Price, 75 cents.

Counter-Currents. A Story. By the author of "Justina." Price, 75 cents.

The Story of Realmah. By SIR ARTHUR HELPS. Price, 75 cents.

The Truth About Clement Ker. A Novel. By GEORGE FLEMING, author of "Kismet," "Mirage," "The Head of Medusa," "Vestigia," "Andromeda." Price, 75 cents.

8. Romances of Real Life. First and Second Series. Selected and Annotated by LEIGH HUNT. Price, 75 cents each.

Religio Medici. A Letter to a Friend, Christian Morals, Urn-Burial, and other Papers. By SIR THOMAS BROWNE. Price, 75 cents.

My Prisons: Memoirs of Silvio Pellico. With a Sketch of his Life by EPES SARGENT. Price, 75 cents.

Wild Life in a Southern County. By RICHARD JEFFERIES, author of "The Gamekeeper at Home," "The Amateur Poacher," "Round about a Great Estate," "The Story of My Heart ; My Autobiography." Price, 75 cents. *"Worthy of a place beside White's 'Selborne.'"*

Deirdrè. A Poem. By ROBERT D. JOYCE. A Romance in Verse which, originally published anonymously in the "No Name Series," created a profound impression. Price, 75 cents.

TORIES OF THE SEEN AND THE UNSEEN,

BY

Mrs. MARGARET O. W. OLIPHANT.

This volume includes the four books hitherto publish
nonymously, viz.: "A Little Pilgrim: In the Unseen;'
The Little Pilgrim: Further Experiences, etc.;" "Old Lad
ary, a Story of the Seen and the Unseen;" "The Ope
oor. The Portrait: Two Stories of the Seen and th
nseen."

One volume. 16mo. Cloth. Price, $1.25.

———◆———

As bits of imaginative writing, Mrs. Oliphant's "Stories of the Seen an
he Unseen" are exquisite productions. The experience of the Little Pilgrin
n her waking in heaven, and her return to earth with her soul filled with th
ght of a Divine beneficence and her mind sure of those higher truths, t
oothe earthly sufferers revolting against the bitterness of loss and pain, ar
old with the sublimated spirituality of one who has just passed through a lon
lness, and whose mind, weak to the impressions of the external world, i
eculiarly sensitive to spiritual visions. No one could have written with mor
octic delicacy of the subjective and objective blessedness of that state o
iture existence which the human heart pictures to itself by the word heaven
nd the story of "Old Lady Mary" will remain a distinct success among tale:
f imaginative literature. — *The Critic.*

We commend the literary delicacy and power of these stories, and ever
ore their tender, stimulating spirituality. — *Congregationalist.*

Deep spiritual truths are given a new beauty; the idea of Divine love anc
eneficence is never lost sight of, and the heart that is filled with sorrow wil
nd in the story of the Little Pilgrim a soothing charm and a something tha
ay heal the scars which have been made by grief and bereavement. — *Phila.
elphia Record.*

———◆———

For sale b   ll

THE WHAT-TO-DO CLUB.
A STORY FOR GIRLS.

By Helen Campbell.

16mo.   Cloth.   Price $1.50.

———◆———

" ' The What-to-do Club ' is an unpretending story. It introduces us to a dozen or more village girls of varying ranks. One has had superior opportunities; another exceptional training; two or three have been ' away to school;' some are farmers' daughters; there is a teacher, two or three poor self-supporters, — in fact, about such an assemblage as any town between New York and Chicago might give us. But while there is a large enough company to furnish a delightful coterie, there is absolutely no social life among them . . . Town and country need more improving, enthusiastic work to redeem them from barrenness and indolence. Our girls need a chance to do independent work, to study practical business, to fill their minds with other thoughts than the petty doings of neighbors. A What-to-do Club is one step toward higher village life. It is one step toward disinfecting a neighborhood of the poisonous gossip which floats like a pestilence around localities which ought to furnish the most desirable homes in our country." — *The Chautauquan.*

" ' The What-to-do Club ' is a delightful story for girls, especially for New England girls, by Helen Campbell. The heroine of the story is Sybil Waite, the beautiful, resolute, and devoted daughter of a broken-down but highly educated Vermont lawyer. The story shows how much it is possible for a well-trained and determined young woman to accomplish when she sets out to earn her own living, or help others. Sybil begins with odd jobs of carpentering, and becomes an artist in woodwork. She is first jeered at, then admired, respected, and finally loved by a worthy man. The book closes pleasantly with John claiming Sybil as his own. The labors of Sybil and her friends and of the New Jersey ' Busy Bodies,' which are said to be actual facts, ought to encourage many young women to more successful competition in the battles of life." — *Golden Rule.*

" In the form of a story, this book suggests ways in which young women may make money at home, with practical directions for so doing. Stories with a moral are not usually interesting, but this one is an exception to the rule. The narrative is lively, the incidents probable and amusing, the characters well-drawn, and the dialects various and characteristic. Mrs. Campbell is a natural story-teller, and has the gift of making a tale interesting. Even the recipes for pickles and preserves, evaporating fruits, raising poultry, and keeping bees, are made poetic and invested with a certain ideal glamour, and we are thrilled and absorbed by an array of figures of receipts and expenditures, equally with the changeful incidents of flirtation, courtship, and matrimony. Fun and pathos, sense and sentiment, are mingled throughout, and the combination has resulted in one of the brightest stories of the season." — *Woman's Journal*

———◆———

Sold by all booksellers.   Mailed, post-paid, by publishers,

MARY W. TILESTON'S SELECTIONS.

Daily Strength for Daily Needs. Selections for every day in the year. 16mo. Plain $1.00
THE SAME. White, gilt 1.25
"   "   Padded calf 3.50
"   "   "   mor. 3.00
Sunshine In the Soul. Poems of Encouragement and Cheerfulness. 16mo. Plain 1.00
THE SAME. White, gilt 1.25
"   "   Padded calf 3.50
"   "   "   mor. 3.00
First and Second Series, separately 50
Quiet Hours. A Collection of Poems. Square 16mo. First and Second Series, each 1 00
THE SAME. Two volumes in one. 16mo 1.50
"   "   White gilt 1.75
"   "   Flexible mor. 3.50
Sursum Corda. Hymns of Comfort. 16mo 1.25
The Blessed Life. Favorite Hymns. Square 18mo 1.00
Classic Heroic Ballads. 16mo. 1 00

WISDOM SERIES.

Issued in handsome pocket volumes. 18mo. Flexible covers, red edges.

Selections from the Apocrypha $0.50
The Wisdom of Jesus, the Son of Sirach; or, Ecclesiasticus 50
Selections from the Thoughts of Marcus Aurelius Antoninus 50
THE SAME. Mor., $1.50; calf 2.50
Selections from the Imitation of Christ 50
Selections from Epictetus 50
THE SAME. Mor., $1.50; calf 2.50
Selections from the Life and Sermons of Tauler .50
Selections from Fénelon. 50
THE SAME. Mor., $1 50; calf 2.50
Socrates. The Apology and Crito of Plato 50
Socrates. The Phædo of Plato 50

Sold by all booksellers. Mailed, postpaid, on receipt of price.

ROBERTS BROTHERS, BOSTON.

THE EARTHLY PARADIS

𝔄 Collection of Tales in Verse.

PARTS I. and II.

PROLOGUE, MARCH, APRIL, MAY, JUNE, JULY, and AUGUST,
containing the Stories of—

The Wanderers.
Atalanta's Race.
The Man born to be King.
The Doom of King Acrisius.
The Proud King.
Cupid and Psyche.

The Writing on the Image.
The Love of Alcestis.
The Lady of the Land.
The Son of Crœsus.
The Watching of the Falcon.
Pygmalion and the Image.

Ogier the Dane

PART III.

SEPTEMBER, OCTOBER, and NOVEMBER, containing the Stories of—

The Death of Paris
The Land East of the Sun and
West of the Moon.
Accontius and Cydippe.

The Man who Never Laughe
Again.
The Story of Rhodope.
The Lovers of Gudrun.

PART IV.

DECEMBER, JANUARY, and FEBRUARY, EPILOGUE, and L'ENVOI,
containing the Stories of—

The Golden Apples.
The Fostering of Aslaug.
Bellerophon at Argos

The Ring given to Venus.
Bellerophon in Lycia.
The Hill of Venus.

COMPLETE IN THREE VOLUMES.

Crown 8vo edition. Green vellum cloth, bevelled boards, gilt t
Price, $6.00. Popular edition. 16mo. Cloth, neat. Price, $4.50.

THE LIFE AND DEATH OF JASON. 16mo. Clo
Price, $1.50.

LOVE IS ENOUGH; OR, THE FREEING OF PHARAMON
A MORALITY. Crown 8vo edition. Green vellum cloth, bevelled boar
gilt top. Price, $2.00. 16mo edition. Cloth, neat. Price, $1.25.

THE DEFENCE OF GUENEVERE, and other Poe
Crown 8vo. Green vellum cloth, bevelled boards, gilt top. Price, $2.

THE STORY OF SIGURD THE VOLSUNG, A
THE FALL OF THE NIBLUNGS. Small 4to. Green vellum clc
gilt top. Price, $2.50.

THE ÆNEIDS OF VIRGIL. Done into English Ver.
Small 4to. Cloth. Price, $2.50.

HOPES AND FEARS FOR ART. 16mo. Clo
Price, $1.25.

THE HOUSE OF THE WOLFINGS. A Tale of t
House of the Wolfings and all the Kindreds of the Mark. Written
Prose and in Verse. Crown 8vo. Cloth. Price, $2.00.

NEWS FROM NOWHERE; OR, AN EPOCH OF RE
Being Some Chapters from a Utopian Romance. 16mo. Clc
Price, $1.00.

PRISONERS OF POVERTY.

WOMEN WAGE-WORKERS: THEIR TRADES AND THEIR LIVES.

By HELEN CAMPBELL,

AUTHOR OF "THE WHAT-TO-DO CLUB," "MRS. HERNDON'S INCOME," "MISS MELINDA'S OPPORTUNITY," ETC.

16mo. Cloth. $1.00. Paper, 50 cents.

The author writes earnestly and warmly, but without prejudice, and her volume is an eloquent plea for the amelioration of the evils with which she deals. In the present importance into which the labor question generally has loomed, this volume is a timely and valuable contribution to its literature, and merits wide reading and careful thought. — *Saturday Evening Gazette.*

She has given us a most effective picture of the condition of New York working-women, because she has brought to the study of the subject not only great care but uncommon aptitude. She has made a close personal investigation, extending apparently over a long time; she has had the penetration to search many queer and dark corners which are not often thought of by similar explorers; and we suspect that, unlike too many philanthropists, she has the faculty of winning confidence and extracting the truth. She is sympathetic, but not a sentimentalist; she appreciates exactness in facts and figures; she can see both sides of a question, and she has abundant common sense. — *New York Tribune.*

Helen Campbell's "Prisoners of Poverty" is a striking example of the trite phrase that "truth is stranger than fiction." It is a series of pictures of the lives of women wage-workers in New York, based on the minutest personal inquiry and observation. No work of fiction has ever presented more startling pictures, and, indeed, if they occurred in a novel would at once be stamped as a figment of the brain. . . . Altogether, Mrs. Campbell's book is a notable contribution to the labor literature of the day, and will undoubtedly enlist sympathy for the cause of the oppressed working-women whose stories do their own pleading. — *Springfield Union.*

It is good to see a new book by Helen Campbell. She has written several for the cause of working-women, and now comes her latest and best work, called "Prisoners of Poverty," on women wage-workers and their lives. It is compiled from a series of papers written for the Sunday edition of a New York paper. The author is well qualified to write on these topics, having personally investigated the horrible situation of a vast army of working-women in New York, — a reflection of the same conditions that exist in all large cities.

It is glad tidings to hear that at last a voice is raised for the woman side of these great labor questions that are seething below the surface calm of society. And it is well that one so eloquent and sympathetic as Helen Campbell has spoken in behalf of the victims and against the horrors, the injustices, and the crimes that have forced them into conditions of living — if it can be called living — that are worse than death. It is painful to read of these terrors that exist so near our doors, but none the less necessary, for no person of mind or heart can thrust this knowledge aside. It is the first step towards a solution of the labor complications, some of which have assumed foul shapes and colossal proportions, through ignorance, weakness, and wickedness. — *Hartford Times.*

Sold by all booksellers. Mailed, post-paid, on receipt of
. . . b th ublishers.

PRISONERS OF POVERTY ABROAD

By HELEN CAMPBELL,

AUTHOR OF "THE WHAT-TO-DO-CLUB," "PRISONERS OF POVERTY,"
"ROGER BERKELEY'S PROBATION," ETC.

16mo. Cloth. Price, $1.00 ; paper, 50 cents.

Mrs. Helen Campbell, an occasional and valued contributor to this journal, and the author of " Prisoners of Poverty," and other studies of social questions in this country, has offered in this book conclusions drawn from investigations on the same themes made abroad, principally in England or France. She has devoted personal attention and labor to the work, and, although much of what she describes has been depicted before by others, she tells her story with a freshness and an earnestness which give it exceptional interest and value. Her volume is one of testimony. She does not often attempt to philosophize, but to state facts as they are, so that they may plead their own cause. She puts before the reader a series of pictures, vividly drawn, but carefully guarded from exaggeration or distortion, that he may form his own opinions. — *Congregationalist.*

Can life be worth living to the hordes of miserable women who have to work from fifteen to eighteen hours a day for a wage of from twenty-five to thirty-five or forty cents? And what have all the study of political economy, all the writing of treatises about labor, all the Parliamentary debates, all the blue books, all the philanthropic organizations, all the appeals to a common humanity, done, in half a century, for these victims of what is called modern civilization? Mrs. Campbell is by no means a sentimentalist. We know of no one who examines facts more coolly and practically, or who labors more earnestly to find the real causes for the continued depression of the labor market, as this horrible state of things is euphemistically termed. The conclusions she reaches are therefore sober and trustworthy.—*New York Tribune.*

No work of fiction, however imaginative, could present more startling pictures than does this little book, which is sympathetic, but not sentimental, the result of personal investigation, and a most valuable contribution to the literature of the labor question. — *Philadelphia Record.*

Mrs. Helen Campbell's " Prisoners of Poverty," a study of the condition of some of the lower strata of the laboring classes, particularly the working-women in the great cities of the United States, is supplemented with another volume, " Prisoners of Poverty Abroad," in which the life of working-women of European cities, chiefly London and Paris, is depicted with equally graphic and terrible truthfulness.

They are the result of fifteen months of travel and study, and are examples of Mrs. Campbell's well-known methods of examination and description. They paint a horrible picture, but a truthful one, and no person of even ordinary sensibilities can read these books without experiencing a strong desire to do something to abate the monstrous injustice which they describe. — *Good Housekeeping.*

STORIES.

AMONA. 5oth thousand . . . . $

EPH. A Posthumous Story . . . .

ERCY PHILBRICK'S CHOICE . . . .

ETTY'S STRANGE HISTORY . . . .

ETWEEN WHILES. A Collection of Stories

TRAVEL.

ITS OF TRAVEL . . . .

ITS OF TRAVEL AT HOME . . . .

LIMPSES OF THREE COASTS . . . .

POEMS.

ERSES BY H. H. 1

ONNETS AND LYRICS. Being a concluding volume of
"Verses" . . . .

ELEN JACKSON'S COMPLETE POEMS. Including "Verses" and "Sonnets and Lyrics." In one volume. 16mo.
White cloth, gilt, $1.75.

CENTURY OF DISHONOR. A Sketch of the United
States Government's Dealings with some of the Indian Tribes.
Seventh edition, enlarged by the addition of the report of the needs
of the Mission Indians of California . . . .

ITS OF TALK ABOUT HOME MATTERS

JUVENILE.

ITS OF TALK FOR YOUNG FOLKS . . . . .

ELLY'S SILVER MINE. A Colorado Story . . . . .

AT STORIES. Comprising "Letters from a Cat," "Mammy
Tittleback and her Family," and "The Hunter Cats of Connorloa."
$2.00; or, separately, $1.25 each.

ROBERTS BROTHERS, Publishers Boston.

CPSIA information can be obtained
at www.ICGtesting.com
Printed in the USA
BVOW05s1057040117

472570BV00007B/202/P